Casting Down of

Strongholds

To Satan and Back

By Kyle D. Frank

Charleston, AR:
COBB PUBLISHING
2019

Published in the United States of America by:
Cobb Publishing
704 East Main St
Charleston, Ark. 72933
www.CobbPublishing.com
CobbPublishing@gmail.com
479-747-8372

Table of Contents

Introduction

The topic of the occult garners a great deal of interest these days—both in our nation and around the world. Different methods of occult practices are seen as "new" and "cutting edge" when, in reality, they are ancient and were practiced by our ancestors back in the distant, dark past. People seem to want that hidden knowledge of the future that God never gave to us. (The word *occult* comes from the Latin word *occultus,* meaning hidden or secret things.) Seekers don't know (or perhaps don't care) that the things which seem so appealing are hazardous. Instead, they just indulge their fascination with the mysterious and the unknown.

Modern society seems to want this unique knowledge any way that they can get it. Nothing is considered as "out of bounds," and no expense is considered too much to reach that knowledge. The entertainment industry thrives on people's hunger to "know the unknowable." Movie studios crank out movies like *Harry Potter* or the *Lord of the Rings* with its wizards and warriors. The box office draws from these movies are nothing short of phenomenal. This is just one area where the magical agenda is furthered by the hunger to know.

Back in the first three centuries of Christianity, there were people just like this. They were called "Gnostics," people who sought "secret knowledge" not given by God. A whole movement followed them. While not an example of the occult, I bring them up as an example of humanity's desire to have "secret knowledge."

People of the world want to have that secret knowledge that God forbade in Deuteronomy 18:9-12. In that, we read:

> *When thou art come into the land which Jehovah thy God giveth thee, thou shalt not learn to do after the abominations of those nations. There shall not be found with thee any one that maketh his son or his daughter to pass through the fire, one that useth divination, one that practiseth augury, or an enchanter, or a sorcerer, or a charmer, or a consulter with a familiar spirit, or a wizard, or a necromancer. For whosoever doeth these things is an abomination unto Jehovah: and be-*

i

cause of these abominations, Jehovah thy God doth drive them out from before thee.

God was clear. This was His business and not ours, and He was unequivocal in condemning it.

This unhealthy fascination is all around us. People are attracted to evil—and that trend only seems to grow as time passes. Things that were done in secret are now seen in the open. It seems that we, as a people, have learned how not to blush. That which was shameful is now celebrated. Until we learn that there are some unacceptable things, we will not get any in better in words and morals. Lord speed the day that we learn.

Although this will be covered in depth in the "Resisting Satan" section, a little needs to be said here on that topic. Our battle here is with forces from somewhere else. We face ancient Principalities and Powers located in the Heavenly, yet according to scripture, they are here on this planet too. Eph. 6:12 mentions this vital topic. We are powerless against them on our own, but because of God the Father, Jesus Christ the Son, and the power of the Holy Spirit, we have become more than victors through Him who loved us.

In our world, there is a tremendous spiritual vacuum caused by the fact that humanity has, for the most part, rejected the true God. Instead, they worship what they like to think of as God. Given the chance to accept or reject the true God, they will refuse because they don't know Him and don't like what they do know about Him, because Satan has so corrupted them that they can't make the right choice. Any choice other than God is a vote for Satan and his sick world civilization. Man crowds into this spiritual vacuum in his life all the moral and ethical values attached to the material world. Lost in a spiritual void, the human heart searches for some reality apart from God and His Word, and discovers the occult "truth" from another dimension.

One thing I've discovered as I've researched this rather morbid topic is the human cost of this war. Yes, freewill gives humanity a choice, but in the vast majority of cases, the person is in bondage (through their own actions and choices) to the evil forces that occupy this world. They are flesh and blood; they are like us. They have a love for one another and have feelings. And most of all, Jesus Christ died for them that they could be made free. The saddest point of all is that they have freedom of choice, and they chose wrong!! They didn't lose their part in humanity, but because of wrong decisions, they will all be lost! It is essential to understand that they are still people of value and worth to God. And all the blasphemy, the anger, and the awful things they may say to you and about Christ, they say in ignorance—precisely like the apostle Paul, who called himself the least of all the apostles, who obtained mercy because he did what he did in ignorance.

Those of us that are, through correct choices, free from this bondage, can thank God—and we should—every day that it wasn't us. We are on the right path, and the word of God tells us so. But, let us strive every day to become what God called us to be. Let us follow these inspired words:

> *So then, my beloved, even as ye have always obeyed, not as in my presence only, but now much more in my absence, work out your own salvation with fear and trembling;* **(Philippians 2:12)**

Salvation is God's gift to man, but we are responsible for our obedience to his commands!

John 14:15*: If ye love me, ye will keep my commandments.*

Let us go forth with love in our hearts, for our Creator first, and then to his creatures as we are able! God gives us strength.

My Story

Chapter One

I have tried on at least three separate occasions to tell the story of our trip through the darkness and into the light, but have failed every time to accurately give an understandable account of what was happening both inside my mind and in our surroundings.

Recently, I received an early answer to prayer when I rediscovered a book that had been long sitting in my library, called "Occult Bondage and Deliverance" by a famous psychologist named Kurt Koch. This gentleman spent his entire life studying the psychological effects of the occult on the human psyche. It can be a hint dry in places, but very rich in experiences and clinical understanding. It helps me explain what was happening in my head during all those years of bondage.

What I didn't realize until very recently was that the vast majority of things these experiences were happening in my mind and personality with just enough supernatural things happening externally to convince us of the reality of the whole mess.

Early Days

In writing a book about the occult, many things must be taken into account. Before talking about the time we were so heavily involved in it, it would probably help to give some of my background, so that those who look at such things will know that I had done things as a youth to encourage it. Granted, I surely was no angel and did my share of misdeeds, but I always wanted to do what was right, even when I was at my worst.

I grew up in a small town in Western New York, about thirty miles south of Buffalo and fifty from Niagara Falls. It was a small community of fewer than one thousand residents. It was very rural, and it was a long drive to anywhere of note. I was born into a family of three boys and two girls. I was the baby of the family, which made me special to my mother, but an object of dislike to my two older brothers, as I was spoiled. My parents divorced when I was three, and my mother remarried a wonderful man when I was six. That man became a second father to me, and I thank him profusely.

In our small community, there were about twenty or so other kids of differing ages. I had plenty of friends with which to play cowboys and war when we were in elementary school. As we grew the 'games' grew, and while we were still in elementary school we learned to smoke by picking up cigarette butts left outside of stores by smokers who could not finish their smoke, and by snitching cigarettes from packs left unguarded around the house. We were also able to get older kids to buy for us, and by the time we reached thirteen, we were regular smokers. Also, in those days—the early 1970's—smoking was not looked down upon. There was no counter-education in school until we reached junior high. By that time, it was too late. We were regular smokers. In High School, I had a competition at BOCES (**B**oard **o**f **C**ooperative **Ed**ucational **S**ervices) with my teacher, who was determined to catch me smoking in the boy's room. I managed to avoid him for two full years. He caught me finally on the last day of my senior year. Because of graduation, they let me go—though I was more than a little concerned.

Another "vice" that was important in our teenage lives was alcohol. That started out with sneaking a glass of beer at a party, and led to getting adults to buy it for us. Also, I was mature-looking for my age and was able to buy it quite often. We would then camp out in the woods or at a friend's barn—anywhere we could find a place to imbibe. We started drinking 'fine' beverages like Pabst Blue Ribbon or Miller High Life or Old Vienna beer. In the early days we were straight beer drinkers, but as we grew, so did our desire for hard liquor or the old stand-by, Mayer Brothers Hard Cider. That was always welcome. It was terrific how ingenious we became in our search for alcohol. By the time I was a freshman in High School, the alcohol consumption had gone from being a sleep-out activity to nightly consumption. Friday and Saturday, I would go to a nearby town (about 15 miles away) where we went to High School, and play along with the band that I was a part of, and the drinks would flow. But by that time, we had progressed to various hard drugs.

During the weeks, when hunting and trapping seasons were in, we would run our traplines and hunt all manner of small game, and of course white-tailed deer. Those could be found in ever-increasing numbers as time passed. We also hunted squirrels and wild turkey when in season. All of these kept us busy, and the trapping brought in money that became funding for our alcohol.

3

We worked on local farms baling hay in the summers. I worked on an Arabian Horse ranch cleaning stalls, carrying hay for the owner's daughter, doing pretty much anything that could be asked. The owner was my English Teacher, so I would ride home from school to work for them. Like most kids of our time, we kept busy and earned money wherever and however we could.

An event which would change my life happened when I was a junior in High School. I started at Erie BOCES where students from six different school districts would be taught a trade. There were Beauticians, Artists, Nursing, Machine Shop, Plastics Technology, and Mechanical Drawing. I went for the last three, which was a "Mechanical Technology" diploma. There were some beautiful things which came from this school, but as one might figure, some terrible things too. Leave it to me to find them quickly. The students, for the most part, were decent, but there was a certain amount of the so-called "dregs of society." I found them quickly. I've heard about like minds attracting. I guess I was acting like a "dreg" myself.

This was where I met and got to know the chaps who were practicing for the pharmaceutical trade. Through this connection, I found myself earning easy money selling drugs while I kept my other jobs as a cover. Also, I made friends with several who were able to use the machines in the shop to manufacture various paraphernalia, which were used by my customers. Unfortunately, I did very well those two years of school, and kept it up until my marriage, when my wife put her foot down on top of mine, and I ended it.

Now, before I go any further, I must say that this is also where I met my wife. She was the lone high point of my time there. She saw me the first day and made a point of "getting to know me." She actively pursued me throughout the two years that I attended BOCES. After we graduated from High School, and I was working a full-time job and had a car, I started seeing her, and one thing led to another, and we were married.

4

And the Story Continues...

Of the writing of many books is called wearisome by the Wiseman of the book of Proverbs. In **Ecclesiastes 12:12**, he says:

> *And furthermore, my son, be admonished: of making many books there is no end, and much study is a weariness of the flesh.*

If this then is a warning against making more books, I must ignore it and continue on this path because of some "experiences" which my young wife and I had early in our now thirty-four-year-old marriage.

I confess that I have two motives for creating this work. **1)** I want to help someone who, like we were, is held in bondage to the occult. Our bondage came through different devices. We used these to attempt to gain knowledge which was forbidden—not only us but to all humankind down throughout history. **2)** Payback. I want to expose Satan for who or what he is and reveal the devices that he uses in his war against God and man. We are the "prize" that he seeks to control so that we will go with him to the Lake of Fire.

What our society and age do not care to know is that we have *all sinned against God* (Romans 3:23), and *the wages of sin is death* (Romans 6:23). Falling into sin is a fatal condition unless you obey Jesus Christ (John 14:15). Having done so, you can know that you have eternal life because of the sacrifice of Jesus Christ on Calvary's cruel cross. He paid for your mistakes.

> *Matthew 11:28-30 Come unto me, all ye that labor and are heavy laden, and I will give you rest. Take my yoke upon you, and learn of me; for I am meek and lowly in heart: and ye shall find rest unto your souls. For my yoke is easy, and my burden is light.*

Our story begins on January 11, 1985, on my twentieth birthday. I was married on my birthday so that I would never forget our anniversary. We were married by the Justice of the Peace in Orchard Park, New York. Like most newlyweds, we were desperately poor and struggled to pay the bills and enjoy the "luxury" of food.

The grand plan was that after we were married, I would leave for boot camp on February 12. We would live on base and start our little family safely and soundly. This would be at Fort Knox. My job was to be a tank mechanic, and Fort Knox is known for other things than gold. It is the foremost armor base, and large numbers of troops are associated with it.

I wrestled with which parts of the story of what boot camp was like and all of my adventures there that I should include here. I will say that I received an injury that put me into Ireland Army Hospital for a period of two weeks. I was injured by following orders that later Command deemed as "trainee abuse." I won't go into it, and I don't think that the Army would appreciate that. Ultimately, I was considered to be as unable to continue—or even start training again (especially as all of my medical records mysteriously disappeared shortly after that). I received a general discharge under the medical heading. So, on April 4 [th], I found myself back in Buffalo, trying to figure out what we were going to do, now that all of our plans were wrecked. A very uncertain future lay before us.

We found a cozy little apartment in Blasdell, NY, about 25 miles from Colden. It was here where we set up house, and eventually, our occult bondage began.

Chapter Two:
Our Journey Through the Darkness

I do not know the exact date when we began using the Ouija board. The idea for making a homemade board came from a book my wife, Jackie, was looking at from the local public library. This library is no longer open, and I don't remember the name of the precise book which enabled us to make a working Ouija board. In appearance, the letters and numbers were small round paper slips taped down on the tabletop of our living-room coffee table. Each slip was about three inches around. There was also the necessary "yes" "no" answers taped to the outside of the table. As a planchette, we used a small glass cup, turned upside-down. It worked surprisingly well for being such a frail-looking thing.

We began on that very first day getting used to "running" that board. After some effort, the planchette seemed to move under its own power. At first, we started with a good number of the usual stupid questions designed to show us precisely WHO was on the other side of that coffee table. It grew in strength and mobility the longer we stayed at it. Soon, besides the "yes" and "no" answers, whatever was using that board was spelling out words at a fast rate. Although we were at first hesitant to do that, the 'other side' was working to make us comfortable using the board. The one thing that should have been a dead-giveaway was that the answers that the board gave us were lies. Over time it lied a lot. At that time, we had no ideas about Satan or demons or virtually anything associated with that board. We still believed (or perhaps hoped) that we were talking to deceased family members and were trying to establish a connection to them. At the end of the night (we did "our thing" from late afternoon until the sun rose the following morning, when we would finally go to bed. Then, the cycle would begin again with the lies and misdirection) we covered the table and went to bed. We followed this schedule for a period of a few weeks. We became so emotionally tied to the board that it was all we wanted to do. Doing this each day, the summer passed by quickly.

The question arises, how can a person fall into Satan's power? Or, putting it in other words, what are the underlying causes of demonic subjection? There are several answers to this question. If a person blatantly lives a life of sin and persistently resists the Spirit of God and remains completely unrepentant, or if a person carries the sin of murder or abortion on his conscience, or has committed perjury or practiced incest, if he has cursed his fellow men or blasphemed against the cross or against Christ, the Holy Spirit, or God, then he will have laid himself open to the devil's attacks. Every curse is, in fact, a cry to the devil, and can, for this reason, lead a person into bondage. But demonic subjection can also arise in the life of a person cursed by someone already in the devil's power. (Occult Bondage and Deliverance, Kurt Koch page 138)

On another day, my wife returned to the library and borrowed an even larger book of the occult with its strange offerings. She spent a great deal of time learning what these various actions meant and if we should try them or not. The one that got my attention was something called "automatic writing," and I took to it like a duck takes to water. My wife tried it first and didn't do so well with it. I, on the other hand, fell in love with it and spent hour upon hour practicing my skills at it.

The best, most straightforward description for automatic writing was to get a pad of paper and a pen. You would position yourself with the pad of paper on a table in front of you. Next, you would totally relax and let the pen sit in your hand with the writing tip resting on a piece of paper. After you relaxed, you would soon begin to feel the pen moving on the paper with no help from you. After a great deal of practice, you could produce many different handwriting styles. Any question that you might ask would receive a reply from the pen.

I still can't imagine who or what was behind this movement and the different handwriting styles that were exhibited. It wasn't Grandma or Uncle Kenny or whoever. I practiced my writing for weeks on end. After a short time doing this, I noticed that somehow, I always knew what the pen-writer was going to say. Whenever we participated in automatic writing events, we did not use the Ouija board, and it eventually fell out of favor to the more straightforward ways of communicating by automatic writing.

> Occult subjection also affects the *character* of the person concerned. As a result of sorcery, one can be plagued by fits of temper and fury, quarrelsomeness, avarice, and a domineering personality. Such people are unsociable and can exhibit all forms of exaggerated passions, including alcoholic addiction and licentiousness. (OBD pg.35)

Well, time passed, and we somehow missed the summer because of our occupation. We would wake around 1 pm and use the board or write to communicate with whatever was talking back to us. We kept at it until sunrise the next morning when the whole process would begin all over.

One day, I had a terrible realization crawl over me. I knew what they were going to say—not because of writing—but because I could hear them in my head. At this point, I became terrified because they were always in my head. As far as I knew, I had no voice in my head, but what I was receiving were thoughts and images of things that were not my own. I had to learn somehow how to "close my mind," so they could not infiltrate my heart or thoughts. I wouldn't say that I heard words, because I know that what I was receiving were thoughts. They were aimed at me every day. But, there was a marked change when I was baptized into the death, burial, and resurrection of the Lord Jesus Christ. The blessed event occurred on Wednesday, August 5, 1987, after the evening Bible class. The gift of the indwelling of God's Holy Spirit, put a complete end to my being bothered by thoughts which were not my own. I struggled with that for many years, but I believe that the Holy Spirit brought the enemy to his defeat on a significant number of battlefields.

I realize that perhaps a great deal of these events sound very strange, but it truly happened. My wife and I have seen "things" in our home many times. But, we don't worry because we know that he that is in the world is far less powerful than He who is in us! We have Jesus Christ as our Savior and elder brother. May we never fail to do good works!

One particular guise in which demonic subjection may appear, is in the form of mediumistic abilities. If this is the case, in addition to the symptoms already mentioned, the subjected person may occasionally fall into a state of unconsciousness (self-hypnosis), or exhibit powers of mesmerism, telepathy or clairvoyance, or walk in his sleep, display extraordinary feats of memory, or develop the ability to use a rod or a pendulum. However, it must be stressed that not all of these symptoms in themselves are necessarily a sign of the demonic. (OBD Page 142)

Having read over this document several times, I realized that one might get the impression that this all happened over a very short period. That is not true at all. These events began when we were playing with a Ouija board in late spring of 1985, and things were occurring up until I was baptized in 1987. That is over two years of living with these things occurring daily. We have seen dark objects in our home; we have seen flashes of light and various other phenomena associated with the occult. On one chilling mid-summer night in 1985, we had decided to call it a day early and go to bed while it was still dark. This led to a tremendous response from whomever or whatever we were in contact with. Our apartment was located on the second floor of the building. While lying in bed, waiting to fall asleep, as folks do on a nightly basis, we were shocked by the sound of someone or something pounding on the <u>outside</u> wall of our building—the outside of a second-story apartment! We ran from room to room, trying to locate the source of the noise. It was a diminutive one-bedroom apartment, and the sound was coming from our own apartment. It sounded like it was in the room that we were in, but it came from the outside of the house!! Those were the sort of things that we lived with in those early days of our marriage.

Another thing previously mentioned was the lies. Now, we *know* that Satan is the father of lies. Back in those days, though, we had no religious knowledge of any type. We did not have a regular Bible, but a small pocket Testament which was given to me by an Army Doctor before I left Ft. Knox in April 1985. So, we were bombarded by lies of every shape and form. I was told blasphemous things that I never gave another thought to—just accepting them as truth. One day, I was told that I was a Son of God as Jesus. So much was piled on that I just took it in stride.

The voices were informing me of what my mission was to be. And I believed them because I did not know God or His works. We were daily fed a steady diet of lies and misinformation. I cannot even begin to express what lies we heard. These all came through the board or by automatic writing. Once we heard that my wife was pregnant, we were told all sorts of things about our baby that would have made a strong man cry. When she was finally born three months early and weighing slightly more than 1 ½ pounds, the lies about her started daily. I don't believe that I ever heard a single statement that was even remotely true outside of my own family and what we knew as truth.

> One of the first things to become subject to the devil's influence is a person's thoughts and feelings. This often results in a complete attitude of indifference to any spiritual influence, and to an open rejection of any belief in God. The Word of God loses its power to speak, and God's promises become meaningless. The person finds he can only entertain evil thoughts in his mind and ideas which are opposed to God. He is gripped with a passion for lying and impure thoughts. Indeed, the desire to lie so fills him that he does so unconsciously. In spite of feeling no remorse for his sins, he will be plagued with a continuous feeling of restlessness, with a lack of peace, and depressive moods. (OBD Page 140)

One thing we never got comfortable with was seeing black forms walk out a door or go through a wall or something similar. They were everywhere, and we could do nothing about it. Around that same time, we began to see what we called "sparkle people," because as we would turn away to go to do something, we would see a flash in the corner of our eyes. That began around that time, and we saw them up till a few years ago when the phenomena ceased. We always wondered what these things meant, but could never find any references to this phenomena. When it came down to it, we were never able to find explanations for anything that had occurred to us or in our house. The one thing that bothered me was that we had since learned that when we began to play around with occult toys, like the board or automatic writing, that we were opening a door that should never have been opened.

I do confess that when we moved we lost track of those spiritual whatever-they-were for at least a short time, then some manifestations appeared but not nearly like before. I fear that we opened a door in that little apartment where we began and then moved away, leaving something horrible for the next tenants to have to deal. Well, we only have the grace and forgiveness of our Blessed Father to lean upon. God is good and so decent, He surely took care of the situation.

One of the experiences that we had with the occult and the near death of our firstborn child came on the third month anniversary of her arrival. She experienced a rupture of her bowel and the most severe occurrence—it could have quickly taken her life before we knew it. Social workers made arrangements for us to stay at the Ronald McDonald house a few streets from the hospital so we could be close while she underwent surgery. We arrived around 9 pm and were escorted to the bedroom where we were going to spend the night.

After the caretaker left, we were a little too wound up to go to sleep, so we talked about the day's events. Suddenly, we both sensed that someone had entered the room. Each of us saw the image in our minds. He was dressed in the attire of a wealthy businessman from the era of about 1830-50. He had the suit on, the hat, and various "airs" about him. More than that, he was very aware that we were in his room and he was not going to tolerate our invasion of his place of repose. He was very hostile to me, and just as much—if not more—to my poor wife, who was under attack by him. He didn't like me being there, but my wife's presence infuriated him without measure. She told me quickly there was someone there who was being hostile to her and that we had to go. I grabbed our bags and made for the door with her hanging on for dear life. Once we escaped, we both began to open up about what had happened. I told her what that "man" looked like as I drove, not noticing that the color had left her cheeks. My description of that man matched perfectly with what she saw.

That night, we took our chances and drove home to Colden and our bed where we could get some sleep. The amazing thing was that the surgery went perfect, and our daughter was the only one unaffected by those terrible times. Today, she is 31 years old and a devout Christian who keeps God's commandments.

> Occultly subjected people frequently begin to show signs of all sorts of *emotional disturbances* when they begin to think about surrendering their lives to Christ. However, we must be very careful to point out at this juncture that emotional illnesses, depressions, neuroses, and suicidal thoughts can have many other causes apart from that of occult involvement. (OBD Page 36)

Another thing that could be talked about was the "personalities" of those beings that were around us during the early to middle time when we were deeply in the occult. They never gave their names, never promised anything, and made our journey far more difficult. What they did was suggest things that were going on around us and tell us what they supposedly meant. We did a lot of research in whatever books we could find that were for those who practiced the occult. No explanation was offered, just a number to contact. I never dared to actually call those numbers we were given by "them."

> Over the years, it has become quite obvious to me through my counseling work that all these mediumistic abilities are really a diabolical counterpart to the spiritual gifts bestowed on us by God. The devil is ever trying to imitate God. One can justify this conclusion by the fact that mediumistic forces and powers can always be overcome and halted through the prayers of a believing Christian. Similarly, the actual possession of mediumistic abilities is always a hindrance to the development of a sound and healthy Christian life. (OBD Page 42)

I spoke earlier of blasphemy, and that is what these characters were. They did not even think about it for a second when it comes to the realm of lies and untruths. I cannot give a decent explanation of how this developed, but we were told that we were special and that I was a Son of God as Jesus Christ. This statement embarrasses me now, but the "guides" were involved in speaking of it. The very worst happening was when I was supposed to do something special, for God. I had so many names and different things that I was supposed to be doing. One day, early in our involvement with the occult, we were told that there were things that we possessed that we could not possess. We were told that we had to get rid of particular possessions—and as much as we disliked the idea, we had to comply, so we did. My wife threw out her high school yearbook, her special clothes, jewelry, and other essential items that she wanted to keep. They were more specific with me. I was told to throw out my high school ring, a yearbook, exercise clothes from when I was in the Army at Ft. Knox, Kentucky, all of my uniforms from BDU's (Battle Dress Uniforms) to my overcoat, which I loved dearly. We kept doing what we were told. We did not know then who this was, but they had revealed enough of themselves that we should have had no doubt. What foolish children we were. All those things were done to us, and we complied. THAT is genuinely being brainwashed.

One thing that is hard to describe is how our daily lives were affected by the occult and the "creatures," which were involved with us daily. I would ask for guidance, and it would surely give it. We had been so brainwashed into believing we were a part of "God's family." Whenever I would bring up the Bible, I was told that it was for other people and did not apply to me. In that way, we were slaves to whatever was controlling us by the Ouija board or automatic writing. Anything we brought up was either explained away or guided away because the Bible wasn't for us but regular people. I had such a feeling towards "Christians" because they were below me in rank and supposed power and physical strength. Oh, how terrible those days were.

All the time, we were being led in a way which kept us away from the way of salvation revealed in the scriptures, or even from any denominational "pastor" who could have pointed us to the Word. All I would need to do is search the scriptures. But I didn't do a single thing to get free. The word "bondage" comes to mind when I think of those days. It has helped me to understand what true bondage is like and that men can be slaves of unseen forces. Even if they look "free," they are not.

At this point, it might help me a bit to say that through all the time that I was a slave to the occult, I just wanted to know God. Something deep down inside of me hungered to know God. Whoever or whatever was our "master" did a great job keeping us away from the "Holy One" and kept our eyes upon the world where we were. We just needed to wait a little longer, and we would receive our "reward" for all that we were doing. Another thing related to us was that Jesus was an "older brother" but was a bit of a screw-up and did not receive any respect from our keepers.

On one particular evening, we were playing with an old tape recorder that we had found somewhere and had learned that it was possible to have a quiet time and ask the tape recorder a question. We would wait for a moment or two, rewind the tape to the start and after we asked a question, listen in to see if someone or something would answer the question. That was seriously frightening because it was actual proof that these things were just not made up in our minds. On that occasion, we asked if anyone was there, left it run a moment, and then rewound the tape and played the most horrifying proof that I could have imagined. The answer was, in a very deep, baritone voice, "Yes, I am here." We played it over and over but could not come up with a good reason to erase it. We held on to this tape until we attended a Memorial Day party at my brother-in-law's house. We played it for him, and he had the same reaction that we did.

We did not do this too many times—at least not intentionally, but had it happen on one particular occasion. We had a portable "Boombox" that we used to record songs that we liked from off of the radio. One favorite song was "Angie," by the Rolling Stones. We started the recording at the beginning and recorded the whole song. When I went to play the recording there were all sorts of voices singing along with "Angie." Most of the voices were horrible sounding. Needless to say, that ended our recording anything any longer. No good could come of that. Like most other things—good, perhaps, in themselves, they were twisted and perverted by our keepers.

At this point, you might be asking why I didn't just turn my back on the occult to live an orderly, demon-free life. The answer is difficult to explain, because we were only 19-21 years of age and had not lived on our own as most "normal" people did. We were little children, playing house with some rather unsavory characters! If you know no difference, how can you decide to change? From what to what?

Change Arrives

Up until now, I have said very little about God or even Jesus Christ. They were supposedly a part of our daily lives that we thought were constant and loving. This was what kept us in bondage. We did not know a single word of the Holy Bible so that, as I said before, was kept just out of our reach. God, being the searcher of thoughts and intents, knew that deep down, we were genuinely looking for Him. We thought that we had arrived in the unique places that were assigned to us. Why leave that? Well, one night, while we were involved with our sessions, my wife began to act in an extraordinary manner. She was 5'1" and about 100 pounds soaking wet. I, at that time, had just gone through U.S. Army bootcamp and was at the absolute peak of my physical conditioning. I was 6'1" and about 190 pounds in weight. I could handle her with absolutely no problem at all. Well, during that session, she began to act far different and had a different facial expression. I wanted her to stay lying down, and she tried to get up. When I figured out that perhaps my honey wasn't quite so sweet, I tried to get her to stay down, but she grabbed my arms like they were nothing and pushed me off of her as though I had been a small child. Her voice, face, eyes had taken on a dark countenance, and she was laughing at my consternation. I felt that there was someone else calling the shots and whoever/whatever it was it was far stronger than I. I was terrified and rolled over on my side of the bed and started calling out for God, not my brutal captor but the true God. The Creator. I was calling out to him out of instinct and with every fiber of my being. Whatever happened, my wife was back, and I kept on calling on Him, who is our rock and salvation. Yeah-that God. I wanted the real thing and I was going to keep calling until He answered me…

Chapter Three:
The Day That Started My Freedom (1)

You would think that a day when I started on the path that led to freedom would be a day when I took the time to sit down and mark it on my calendar! But that wasn't me. When that day came, I was so deeply buried in the occult that I could not manage to lift my head enough to know what day of the month it was. It was a beautiful Sunday morning in the springtime of 1986. That is as close as I can remember. My wife and I had been through our usual night of lurking around in our "lovely" occult areas, lying and being lied to. Life was as it had been since our entrapment in 1985.

On this Sunday morning, there was a soft tapping at the door. We did not know anyone there, and no one knew us, so we were both a little apprehensive as to whom it could be. I opened the door—in my bathrobe—and there was this well-dressed elderly man and his wife. They were both very friendly and polite. The man introduced himself as Joe and his wife as Angie. They produced a correspondence course that I had seen in the local newspaper and asked for. This was the very start of my new life, a life of freedom and love that could only have come from God Almighty. This was after my repeated prayers of "Where are you?" during one of our occult situations. They became my parents in the gospel, and I love them as deeply as if they had been my physical parents.

That prayer had an instantaneous answer, it seems, as the newspaper ad showed up that day. As soon as they left, I launched out into the clear, cold, refreshing water of the gospel, leaving behind the fetid, bilge water of the occult. Sewage is a more apt description. I could have done the study all in one sitting, but my teacher insisted on slowing down. He couldn't understand what we had been through, didn't realize that, spiritually, I was deathly ill and needed the medicine that could only come from the gospel. I did manage to get him to do two studies with me. The correspondence course was an eight-lesson course by John Hurt, and our studies were in a class produced by Ivan Stewart called "Open Bible Study."

Joe and I met during the day while Angie held down a full-time job. We had plenty of time, and we used it well. The very first two questions hit hard at my occult moorings.

The verse was:

> **2 Peter 1:3**: *seeing that his divine power hath granted unto us all things that pertain unto life and godliness, through the knowledge of him that called us by his own glory and virtue.*

The questions were:

> **Yes — No** Has God given us everything we need for life and godliness?
>
> **Yes — No** Since "all" has been provided, do you need additional information other than the Bible?

These two questions were like taking an ax to an ugly tree. I couldn't believe the implications. I didn't need everything—no, I didn't need *anything* that I had been told by our handlers. Now if this came from just the first question of the first study, what else lay ahead? I could hardly wait to find out!

> **Ephesians 2:15** *having abolished in his flesh the enmity, even the law of commandments contained in ordinances; that he might create in himself of the two one new man, so making peace;*
>
> **Colossians 2:13-14** *who delivered us out of the power of darkness, and translated us into the kingdom of the Son of his love; in whom we have our redemption, the forgiveness of our sins:*

> **Yes — No** Has God abolished the law with its commandments and regulations?
>
> **Yes — No** Were the hand-written ordinances (Ten Commandments) taken out of the way at the time Jesus died on the cross?

More shocks to my occultic system—these were questions I had that our dark "guides" would not answer.

Hebrews 8:6-7 But now hath he obtained a ministry the more excellent, by so much as he is also the mediator of a better covenant, which hath been enacted upon better promises. For if that first covenant had been faultless, then would no place have been sought for a second.

Yes — No Does God contrast the two covenants: the law of Moses and the New Testament of Christ?

Yes — No If nothing had been wrong with the law of Moses, would God have replaced it with the law of Christ?

Romans 7:6-7 But now we have been discharged from the law, having died to that wherein we were held; so that we serve in newness of the spirit, and not in oldness of the letter. What shall we say then? Is the law sin? God forbid. Howbeit, I had not known sin, except through the law: for I had not known coveting, except the law had said, Thou shalt not covet

Yes — No Are you delivered (discharged/released) from the law?

Yes — No Since you are released from the law of Moses (including the Ten Commandments), should you serve that law?

2 Timothy 3:16-17: Every scripture inspired of God is also profitable for teaching, for reproof, for correction, for instruction which is in righteousness: that the man of God may be complete, furnished completely unto every good work.

Yes — No Since the Scriptures make known the will of God to thoroughly equip (furnish) you for every good work, do you need other revelations to make you complete spiritually?

Yes — No Is it your understanding that the New Testament is the law now spiritually binding?

Another **blockbuster**! The New Testament gives us everything that we could need—incredible! The cord between Satan and me was being cut at such a rate that I had never imagined could happen.

Looking back, I see that, as some would say, "the gig was up" when I started looking at holy things. I did not own a full Bible, but I made a point of looking at them when I could, which was 'conveniently' not often, due to my circumstances. I was 'encouraged' to buy a copy of "The Book," which isn't a Bible at all, but it was encouraged by my handlers as a "great Bible" to learn from. What a recommendation—being inspired by a demon to buy a so-called "Bible." What does that say about "The Book?"

> **John 12:48:** *He that rejecteth me, and receiveth not my sayings, hath one that judgeth him: the word that I spake, the same shall judge him in the last day.*
>
> **Yes — No** Will the words of Jesus judge you in the last day, rather than the words or commandments of Moses or others?

This blew my mind because I had been taught that I was a Son-of-God, brother to Jesus Christ, and he was going to judge me? I had been exempt (so I thought) until I started studying God's word for a day, and was utterly crushed, but I had hope—something I had not had in over two years! Hope is a beautiful thing.

> **John 10:10** *The thief cometh not, but that he may steal, and kill, and destroy: I came that they may have life and may have it abundantly.*
>
> **Yes — No** Did Jesus come so that you could have a full and abundant life now, as well as in eternity?

> **John 14:6** *Jesus saith unto him, I am the way, and the truth, and the life: no one cometh unto the Father, but by me*
>
> **Yes — No** Since Jesus said He came to give a full and abundant life, should you go to Jesus' words (teachings) to learn of His way to have that life?

Yes — No Could the words of these people give you the abundant life: mothers, fathers, husbands, wives, friends, or neighbors?

Yes — No Could the words of these people give you the abundant life: Joseph Smith, John Calvin, Martin Luther, Wesley Brothers, John Knox or the Pope?

Matthew 7:13-14 Enter ye in by the narrow gate: for wide is the gate, and broad is the way, that leadeth to destruction, and many are they that enter in thereby.

Yes — No Will the majority enter heaven?

Yes — No Is the majority a safe guide for your spiritual life?

Yes — No Do you want to go to heaven?

Matthew 7:21-23 Not every one that saith unto me, Lord, Lord, shall enter into the kingdom of heaven; but he that doeth the will of my Father who is in heaven. Many will say to me in that day, Lord, Lord, did we not prophesy by thy name, and by thy name cast out demons, and by thy name do many mighty works? And then will I profess unto them, I never knew you: depart from me, ye that work iniquity.

Yes — No Since Jesus said He came to give a full and abundant life, should you go to Jesus to learn of His way to have that life?

Yes — No Did Jesus say you could enter heaven by doing the will of men?

Yes — No Could Jesus say, "Depart from me," even if you are sincere and say, "Lord, Lord" and do many good works?

Matthew 28:20 *teaching them to observe all things whatsoever I commanded you: and lo, I am with you always, even unto the end of the world.*

Yes — No Did Jesus say that you could observe part of His will and still please Him?

Yes — No Is it your understanding that you must do "all of the wills of God" to please Him?

John 3:16 *For God so loved the world, that he gave his only begotten Son, that whosoever believeth on him should not perish, but have eternal life.*

Yes — No Is it God's will that you believe in Jesus?

John 8:24 *I said therefore unto you, that ye shall die in your sins: for except ye believe that I am he, ye shall die in your sins.*

John 14:15 *If ye love me, ye will keep my commandments.*

Matthew 22:37-38 *And he said unto him, Thou shalt love the Lord thy God with all thy heart, and with all thy soul, and with all thy mind. This is the great and first commandment.*

Yes — No Is it God's will that you believe in Christ AND love Him?

Yes — No If you do not obey Christ, do you love Him?

Romans 6:17 *But thanks be to God, that, whereas ye were servants of sin, ye became obedient from the heart to that form of teaching whereunto ye were delivered*

Yes — No When you obey God can you obey only from an outward expression and not from the heart?

Yes — No When you obey God, must you follow God's "form of teaching?"

Luke 13:3 *I tell you, Nay: but, except ye repent, ye shall all in like manner perish.*

Yes — No In addition to belief and love, is it God's will that you repent?

Yes — No Will, you receive the full and abundant life if you do not repent?

Acts 3:19 *Repent ye therefore, and turn again, that your sins may be blotted out, that so there may come seasons of refreshing from the presence of the Lord;*

2 Cor. 7:10 *For godly sorrow worketh repentance unto salvation, a repentance which bringeth no regret: but the sorrow of the world worketh death.*

Yes — No Does repentance mean to stop sinning and turn to God?

Matthew 10:32-33 *Every one therefore who shall confess me before men, him will I also confess before my Father who is in heaven. But whosoever shall deny me before men, him will I also deny before my Father who is in heaven.*

Yes — No In addition to belief, love, AND repentance, is it God's will that you should confess/acknowledge Christ before men?

Romans 10:9-10 *because if thou shalt confess with thy mouth Jesus as Lord, and shalt believe in thy heart that God raised him from the dead, thou shalt be saved: for with the heart man believeth unto righteousness, and with the mouth confession is made unto salvation.*

Yes — No Will, you be saved if you do not confess Jesus with your mouth before men?

That finished off my dreams of being Christ's "brother." Now I had to follow directions. What a change. It was all over with; my occultic dreams were crushed once and for all.

Those were just a few of the questions and answers on the very first lesson. It was the most memorable event of my life. I was only 22 years old, but I was going to have to do some growing up quickly. I was amazed at how Satan's "power" just melted in the presence of God, THE God of all. It makes me remember to praise him all the more. More will be covered in the next couple of lessons. I hope that you enjoy it as much as I have enjoyed telling it.

Chapter Four:
The Day That Started My Freedom (2)

All the time that I was studying the John Hurt course at home and studying the Open Bible Study course with Joe and Angie, I was reading the New Testament, trying to learn as much as I could from all three sources. I sensed the freedom that was in Christ and hungered for it as I had never hungered for anything before. Jesus did say Matthew 5:6 *Blessed are they that hunger and thirst after righteousness: for they shall be filled.* I didn't understand what he was saying, but I believed it, whatever it was. Thankfully I had lost the false idea that I was another son of God like Jesus and had gratefully accepted my position as a lowly learner. I knew that I wasn't a disciple yet, though I so wanted to be. Amazing, how I went from "a Son of God" to a lowly disciple wannabe so quickly and easily, but life all depends upon your attitude.

I had an NIV New Testament that Joe and Angie so generously purchased for me, and that horrible thing called "The Book" that I had been "directed" to get by my "handlers." It was a very watered-down paraphrase of the Bible, that the voices hoped would keep me occupied instead of reading an actual Bible. I ended up reading the NIV all the time because it had verses in it and looked more like the Bible that Joe read.

Lesson #2 began with a blockbuster:

> *Matt. 16:15-17 He saith unto them, But who say ye that I am? And Simon Peter answered and said, Thou art the Christ, the Son of the living God. And Jesus answered and said unto him, Blessed art thou, Simon Bar-Jonah: for flesh and blood hath not revealed it unto thee, but my Father who is in heaven.*

Yes — No Was Jesus pleased with Peter's acknowledgement (confession)?

Yes — No Will Christ be pleased if you make the same confession today?

Yes — No Can you be saved by desiring only— believing only — confessing Christ only?

25

This scripture made me remember who Jesus really was and not the goofy older brother the "minders" made me think that he was. It was unraveling faster now. I had it right there in the Bible that it was so. 2 Timothy 3:16-17 had taught me that.

> **Mark 15:15-16** *And he said unto them, Go ye into all the world, and preach the gospel to the whole creation. He that believeth and is baptized shall be saved; but he that disbelieveth shall be condemned.*

Yes— No Is salvation promised to those who believe AND are baptized?

Yes — No In addition to believing — loving — repenting — confessing — is it God's will that you be baptized?

> **Romans 6:23; Ezekiel 18:4** *(verses too long to print)*

Yes — No If you do not receive "remission of sins" can you enjoy God's gift of eternal life?

> **Acts 2:37-47; 22:16**

Yes — No Did these sinners gladly accept the word and obey the command to be baptized?

Yes — No Were their sins forgiven at baptism?

Yes — No Did the Lord add to their number (the church) daily those who were being saved?

> **Ephesians 4:4-5**: *There is one body, and one Spirit, even as also ye were called in one hope of your calling; one Lord, one faith, one baptism.*

Yes — No Is there more than one valid baptism in God's will?

I remember sitting at the table in Angie's dining room and reading that verse. Joe began to talk about the one baptism. It hit me, hard. I suddenly realized that my baptism in 1965 as an infant meant **nothing**. I was still in my sins! I was still lost. I remember 32 years ago, the sensation of feeling my blood run cold—ice cold. I began to stammer as I tried to explain to Joe my utter terror, and that we needed to get to the building—which I had never been to as of yet—so I could get baptized and safe. What an awful feeling. I was in real danger. I couldn't understand Joe's faith as of yet (and he was right, of course), when he said that the Lord had protected me to that lovely day. I was a long time getting over that.

Acts 8:35-39

Yes — No Did the eunuch desire to be baptized in water?

Yes — No Did Philip take the eunuch down into the water and bring him up out of the water?

Yes — No Was water sprinkled on the eunuch?

Romans 6:3-4 *Or are ye ignorant that all we who were baptized into Christ Jesus were baptized into his death? We were buried therefore with him through baptism into death: that like as Christ was raised from the dead through the glory of the Father, so we also might walk in newness of life.*

Yes — No Was Paul baptized/buried/immersed in the same manner as the eunuch in Acts 8:35-39?

Yes — No Are those who are baptized in the same manner as the eunuch and Paul doing God's will?

Yes — No Will you please God if you are not immersed for the forgiveness of your sins

Colossians 3:17 *And whatsoever ye do, in word or in deed, do all in the name of the Lord Jesus, giving thanks to God the Father through him.*

Yes — No In addition to believing — loving — repenting — confessing Christ and being baptized, is it God's will that you do "all" in the "name of the Lord" rather than the name of some man?

John 17:21 *that they may all be one; even as thou, Father, art in me, and I in thee, that they also may be in us: that the world may believe that thou didst send me.*

    Yes — No Does Jesus want His followers to be "one?"

1 Corinthians 1:10-13 *Now I beseech you, brethren, through the name of our Lord Jesus Christ, that ye all speak the same thing, and that there be no divisions among you; but that ye be perfected together in the same mind and in the same judgment. For it hath been signified unto me concerning you, my brethren, by them that are of the household of Chloe, that there are contentions among you. Now this I mean, that each one of you saith, I am of Paul; and I of Apollos; and I of Cephas; and I of Christ. Is Christ divided? was Paul crucified for you? or were ye baptized into the name of Paul?*

Yes — No Does the Lord approve of denominationalism and wearing different names religiously?

Yes — No Does the Lord rebuke those who speak different things religiously from what Jesus and the apostles spoke?

Yes — No If Group A believes that people are saved by "faith only" and Group B believes that people "must believe, repent, confess and be baptized," should both change in order to speak the "same thing?"

Yes — No Does the Lord approve of "Apollosite Christians" or "Paulite Christians?"

1 Cor. 3:4-5 *for ye are yet carnal: for whereas there is among you jealousy and strife, are ye not carnal, and do ye not walk* *after the manner of men? For when one saith, I am of Paul; and another, I am of Apollos; are ye not men? What then is Apollos? and what is Paul? Ministers through whom ye believed; and each as the Lord gave to him.*

Yes — No Would it be a sin for you to say, "I am of Paul" or "I am of_____"

Ephesians 4:4; 1:22-23

Yes — No Does the Bible reveal there is but one body (church) just as there is one Lord?

Another absolute blockbuster—God doesn't approve of all these other churches, "Worship at the church of your choice." Sounds good, but it isn't in God's Word, so it must be rejected. The idea that I needed to learn was that the Bible is from the mind of God, and in it, we find his will. We don't have the right to make our own choices. This is God's show, and we must obey Him if we want to be with Him. His world, His will. We just need to be thankful that He wanted us to be there enough to make a way for it to happen.

Colossians 1:18 *And he is the head of the body, the church: who is the beginning, the firstborn from the dead; that in all things he might have the preeminence.*

Yes — No Should Jesus, as head of the body, the church, receive first place of honor and supremacy including the name His followers wear?

Matt. 16:18 *And I also say unto thee, that thou art Peter, and upon this rock I will build my church; and the gates of Hades shall not prevail against it.*

Yes — No Did Jesus promise to build many churches?

Yes — No Did Jesus promise to build His (possessive) church

Jesus never promised to create several churches. He only said one only, so we have to accept and obey that.

> ***Acts 2:47; 22:16*** *And now why tarriest thou? arise, and be baptized, and wash away thy sins, calling on his name.*
>
> **Yes — No** Did these sinners gladly accept the word and obey the command to be baptized?
>
> **Yes — No** Were their sins forgiven at baptism?
>
> **Yes — No** Did the Lord add to their number (the church) daily?

Baptism again—but at least I see how very vital that it is in the divine economy!! It was nearly the last thing to do, but it was so important to God, which made it essential for me. All I could do was study and pray about it.

> ***John 6:53-54****: Jesus, therefore, said unto them, Verily, verily, I say unto you, Except, ye eat the flesh of the Son of man and drink his blood, ye have not life in yourselves. He that eateth my flesh and drinketh my blood hath eternal life: and I will raise him up at the last day.*
>
> **Yes — No** If you fail to partake of the total teachings of Christ, which includes the Lord's Supper, will you be entitled to eternal life?

That last question was a complete shock to me as I was not prepared for the totality of following Christ. I found out that as you grew, it became easier to follow. Now, as I have matured, it is natural.

The path to Christ was not an easy one, but when compared to the occult, it was a dream — no longer being lied to and misled made things so much better. But, we still experienced some of the manifestations that we had when we were in the depths of bondage. The physical signs, such as the dark figures in hallways walking about were still there, though greatly diminished. I still experienced their thoughts when I was not expecting it. The vulgarity was indeed even there, and intrusions into prayers were again happening from time to time. You might think these to be excessive, but we yet had not been baptized and therefore were still in the world. I focused on the gracious things God had done and spent more time in prayer.

All in all, life was good and getting better. The more time that I spent in the Word of God, the stronger I got and the weaker they became. If I had only come across 2 Corinthians 10:3-6,

> *For though we walk in the flesh, we do not war according to the flesh (for the weapons of our warfare are not of the flesh, but mighty before God to the casting down of strongholds), casting down imaginations, and every high thing that is exalted against the knowledge of God, and bringing every thought into captivity to the obedience of Christ,*

I would have understood the nature of the battle much to my advantage. But, all's well that ends well!

Chapter Five:
The Day That Started My Freedom (3)

The journey toward total forgiveness was so slow that I almost couldn't bear it. I tried so hard to appear patient when Joe and Angie were around, but inwardly I just wanted to jump in a creek. I knew that water was part of the plan, but at this point, jumping into a creek is all would have been, because I did not understand the plan of salvation yet. It's hard to be patient when you realize you need to be saved!

We were still being bothered with apparitions and what we came to call the "sparkle people," a small flash of brilliant white light at the edge of our field of view. Sometimes only one of us, but often both of us would see the same phenomena at the same time. The light was (and I know this sounds strange) whiter than white.

Lesson three of the OBS started.

Acts 20:7 And upon the first day of the week, when we were gathered together to break bread, Paul discoursed with them, intending to depart on the morrow; and prolonged his speech until midnight.

Yes — No Did the First Century Christians partake of the Lord's Supper on Sunday, the first day of the week?

Yes — No Should Christians in this Century partake of the Lord's Supper on any other day?

Pretty clear.

1 Cor. 16:1-2 Now concerning the collection for the saints, as I gave order to the churches of Galatia, so also do ye. Upon the first day of the week, let each one of you lay by him in store, as he may prosper, that no collections be made when I come.

Yes — No Were the Christians in Corinth admonished to contribute (collection of money) on the same day as Christians in Troas (Acts 20:7) partook of the Lord's Supper?

Yes — No Is it your understanding that it is the Lord's will to love—believe—repent—confess Christ—be baptized—do all in the name of Christ—partake of the Lord's Supper and make a contribution on the first day of each week?

This question gave me a lot to think about. There was the plan, but I didn't know whether there was more.

Heb 10:25 not forsaking our own assembling together, as the custom of some is, but exhorting one another; and so much the more, as ye see the day drawing nigh.

Yes — No Is it the Lord's will for you to be absent from the assembly of the saints?

Yes — No Can you worship God with the saints if you are not present when Christians meet?

I admit that I struggled with attendance at first, but with growth, that got better.

Acts 2:42 And they continued steadfastly in the apostles' teaching and fellowship, in the breaking of bread and the prayers.

Yes — No Were the First Century Christians steadfast in their devotion and service to God?

Yes — No Should you be so devoted and steadfast today?

That devotion only grows with age. It is a beautiful thing.

2 Tim. 2:15 Give diligence to present thyself approved unto God, a workman that needeth not to be ashamed, handling aright the word of truth.

Yes — No Does God want you to correctly handle the word of God which requires diligent study?

Philippians 1:9 *And this I pray, that your love may abound yet more and more in knowledge and all discernment.*

Yes — No Is it God's will that you continue to grow spiritually?

1 Thessalonians 5:17 *pray without ceasing*

Yes — No Is it God's will that Christians pray continually?

Ephesians 5:19 *speaking one to another in psalms and hymns and spiritual songs, singing and making melody with your heart to the Lord.*

Colossians 3:16 *Let the word of Christ dwell in you richly; in all wisdom teaching and admonishing one another with psalms and hymns and spiritual songs, singing with grace in your hearts unto God.*

Yes — No Does the New Testament teach that you should sing and make music "in your heart" to the Lord?

Yes — No Do these passages mention a mechanical instrument of music?

Yes — No When you "sing" and "make music in the heart" should you also "teach," "admonish" and "speak?"

The next part of the study really shook me. It scared me. Badly. It took a lot of time for me to fully wrap my head around it, and understand the implications. Because if this was true, I was about to have to fight the battle of my life against the voices, the handlers—the demonic forces that were trying to influence me.

34

Revelation 22:18-19 *I testify unto every man that heareth the words of the prophecy of this book, If any man shall add unto them, God shall add unto him the plagues which are written in this book: and if any man shall take away from the words of the book of this prophecy, God shall take away his part from the tree of life, and out of the holy city, which are written in this book.*

1 Corinthians 4:6 *Now these things, brethren, I have in a figure transferred to myself and Apollos for your sakes; that in us ye might learn not to go beyond the things which are written; that no one of you be puffed up for the one against the other.*

Deuteronomy 4:2 *Ye shall not add unto the word which I command you, neither shall ye diminish from it, that ye may keep the commandments of Jehovah your God which I command you.*

Yes — No Does the Lord desire that <u>anything be added to His word</u>?

Yes — No Does the Lord desire that <u>anything be taken away from His word</u>?

Yes — No Would you please the Lord if you added steak and cake to the Lord's Table or a piano or organ to the singing of praises to God?

My blood ran cold when I finally grasped the significance of the verses I had just read. By listening to whatever was talking to me, I was trying to add something to God's commands, not to mention that they encouraged me to not follow other commands—I was violating both sides of the "adding and taking away" command.

Please, dear reader, understand this: adding to or taking away from the word of God is something that will cost you your soul. This is not a topic to be taken lightly! It is definitely worth the time to understand clearly.

Galatians 1:8 But though we, or an angel from heaven, should preach unto you any gospel other than that which we preached unto you, let him be anathema.

Yes — No If anyone preaches a gospel that cannot be read in the New Testament, will he be eternally condemned?

Yes — No Since your soul's destination depends on what you obey, would you want your best friend to preach anything to you other than that which can be read in the New Testament?

I remember realizing at that time that "The Book" (the paraphrase that the handlers suggested I use) was not the gospel, and I got rid of it very quickly. I am still skeptical of even many "proper" translations (that is, actual translations instead of paraphrases), and won't use a vast majority of them. I refuse to risk my soul by following translations that give anything other than the actual words of Scripture. I see these wrong translations of the scriptures as just like rat poison mixed with healthy food. I destroy that material as I get ahold of it.

Romans 12:1-2 I beseech you therefore, brethren, by the mercies of God, to present your bodies a living sacrifice, holy, acceptable to God, which is your spiritual service. And be not fashioned according to this world: but be ye transformed by the renewing of your mind, that ye may prove what is the good and acceptable and perfect will of God.

Yes — No Should Christians present themselves as living sacrifices to the service of God?

We are to be living sacrifices for God because He gave His son to be a sacrifice for us. Plain and simple!

Titus 2:12-14 instructing us, to the intent that, denying ungodliness and worldly lusts, we should live soberly and righteously and godly in this present world; looking for the blessed hope and appearing of the glory of the great God and our Savior Jesus Christ; who gave himself for us, that he might redeem us from all iniquity, and purify unto himself a people for his own possession, zealous of good works

Yes — No Are you, as a follower of the Lord, permitted to live unrighteously or as you please?

We MUST remember that we were bought with a price—the highest price ever—and that we must follow the Lord by whatever means He has determined, and do it without complaining and murmuring. Eternity depends upon it!!

Rev. 2:10 *Fear not the things which thou art about to suffer: behold, the devil is about to cast some of you into prison, that ye may be tried; and ye shall have tribulation ten days. Be thou faithful unto death, and I will give thee the crown of life.*

Yes — No Must you be faithful unto death in order to be saved eternally?

James 4:17 *To him therefore that knoweth to do good, and doeth it not, to him it is sin.*

Yes — No Will it do you any good to know to do God's will, and then not do it?

Yes — No Should you obey all of God's will?

Not only know it but DO it to be saved. Obedience is Everything! My heart rate was picking up as we continued through the questions. I was anxious to obey!

John 14:15 *If ye love me, ye will keep my commandments.*

Yes — No , Will you keep the commands of Christ if you love him?

37

This scripture pops into my mind ten times a day-it seems.

> ***Acts 22:16*** *And now why tarriest thou? arise, and be baptized, and wash away thy sins, calling on his name.*

> **Yes — No** Was Paul commanded to obey the Lord immediately? Are we?

That was the last straw for me. I was in the water within a few days. That was as quick as I could get it.

> ***2 Corinthians 6:2*** *for he saith, At an acceptable time I hearkened unto thee, And in a day of salvation did I succor thee: behold, now is the acceptable time; behold, now is the day of salvation*

> ***James 4:14*** *whereas ye know not what shall be on the morrow. What is your life? For ye are a vapor that appeareth for a little time, and then vanisheth away.*

> When should you obey the will of God?

This lesson brought me to the end of the study with a decision to make. Obey Christ Jesus and to live according to his commands, or reject him and stay with what I knew, what was comfortable.

After the information I had received and meditated upon, the question was an easy one—to obey and live, or not obey and die in my sins. Although my physical life continues, the old life ended in the pool of baptism on Wednesday night, August 5th, 1987. What a glorious night that was. Freedom, forgiveness, acceptation, and love. Yes, like all, I have slipped and fallen in the mud of sin, yet, being given the gift of repentance and forgiveness, the glorious life of fellowship with God carries on each and every day because of that simple gift that God gave on that horrible cross around A.D. 33 when Jesus Christ said, "It is finished." And it was.

Resisting Satan

Chapter Six:
The Spiritual Battle[1]

This world is a place of great physical beauty, but spiritually it is a very dark place. This world is a battlefield where the forces of good and the forces of evil are striving for victory against one another. Here, the kingdom of Satan strives for mastery against the kingdom of God. It has been so since the serpent tricked Eve into eating the fruit of the tree of knowledge of good and evil. When that happened, there was no way to undo the damage. Thankfully, God had a plan in mind to rescue us from our sins. This plan was in God's mind before he created us. It was in his mind before he created the earth.

Being both physical and spiritual beings, we are drawn into the fight, and we must always keep in mind that it is a real battle with a real enemy. Hollywood has put into the minds of many a carnal, physical enemy, with movies like "The Omen" and "The Exorcist." Yes, at times, we do face those who have evil intent, but we need to remember that the forces behind those people and actions are the evil one and his minions. The real battle is a spiritual one, and we need to remember that those people we face are merely tools doing the bidding of those behind the scenes.

The Bible has much to tell us about this war. It is a battle for our souls and is in the "heavenly places." The book of Ephesians is replete with references to this struggle. In chapter 1:3, we see:

> *Blessed be the God and Father of our Lord Jesus Christ, who hath blessed us with every spiritual blessing in the <u>heavenly places</u> in Christ.*

Verse 20 further says:

> *which he wrought in Christ when he raised him from the dead and made him to sit at his right hand in the <u>heavenly places</u>.*

Chapter 2:6 says:

---

[1] (It is at this part that I thank Rob Harbison profusely for supplying me with a skeletal outline on which I wrote this. Thank You Again, Rob!!!)

*and raised us up with him and made us to sit with him in the
<u>heavenly places</u>, in Christ Jesus.*

Chapter 3:10 tells us:

*to the intent that now unto the principalities and the powers in
the <u>heavenly places</u> might be made known through the church,
the manifold wisdom of God.*

And finally, 6:12:

*For our wrestling is not against flesh and blood, but against
the principalities, against the powers, against the world-rulers
of this darkness, against the spiritual hosts of wickedness in
the <u>heavenly places</u>.*

To lay this out, we see that:
1. Our blessings are in heavenly places.
2. We sit with him in the heavenly places
3. The principalities and powers and world-rulers are also in
   heavenly places.
4. We wrestle with those entities in the heavenly places and
   that our warfare is not primarily with flesh and blood.

This warfare is not in the future but is going on NOW. We actively participate in this while our physical bodies are in this physical world. It might sound a little strange, but God's word, given
by God's Spirit, is clear on this subject. There is no "well, I think
that..." but instead a "thus saith the Lord." We need to accept this,
just as we have accepted the fact that Christ died on our behalf and
was raised by the power of the Father.

What is Satan fighting for? What could be the reason for all of
this strife and contention? What is going to happen as a result of
this hostility? Let us look back to the pages of God's word for the
answer. John 12:31 tells us that:

*Now is the judgment of this world: now shall the prince of this
world be cast out.*

In 1 John 5:19, we are told:

*We know that we are of God and the whole world lieth in the
evil one.*

What is he fighting for? He might have the whole world under his power, but why fight a losing battle? This has been a subject that many writers have struggled with. I will share what I do know, and perhaps that will shed some light on the subject. Regarding Satan:

1. We should never speak contemptuously about him (Jude, verse 6). Even the angels, who are much higher than we are *durst not bring against him a railing judgment, but said, The Lord rebuke thee.*

2. We should regard Satan's power as limited.

> ***Job 1:12*** *And Jehovah said unto Satan, Behold, all that he hath is in thy power; only upon himself put not forth thy hand. So Satan went forth from the presence of Jehovah.*

> ***Job 2:6-7*** *And Jehovah said unto Satan, Behold, he is in thy hand; only spare his life. So Satan went forth from the presence of Jehovah and smote Job with sore boils from the sole of his foot unto his crown.*

In each of these instances, Satan had to get permission from God to do anything against Job. Though his power is limited, we should realize that on our own—without the overwhelming power that is in Jesus Christ—we are no match for him. Our strength is as nothing when compared to the great evil one. We should walk in a spirit of humility and not utter these great swelling boasts that are often seen coming from the ungodly. Some of these are seen in the book of Psalms.

> ***Psalm: 49:6:*** *They that trust in their wealth and boast themselves in the multitude of their riches;*

> ***94:4*** *They prate, they speak arrogantly: All the workers of iniquity boast themselves;*

> ***97:7:*** *Let all them be put to shame that serve graven images, That boast themselves of idols: Worship him, all ye gods.*

In the New Testament, we see two examples:

> ***2 Peter 2:18*** *For, uttering great swelling words of vanity, they entice in the lusts of the flesh, by lasciviousness, those who are just escaping from them that live in error*

Jude 16: *These are murmurers, complainers, walking after their lusts (and their mouth speaketh great swelling words), showing respect of persons for the sake of advantage.*

3. We need to remember that the Lord's work and word protect us. John 17:15 says:

I pray not that thou shouldest take them from the world, but that thou shouldest keep them from the evil one.

1 John 2:14 also says that we have overcome the evil one. By Christ's power, that is possible.

4. We must remember that Satan is a judged and defeated foe. John 16:11 tells us:

of judgment because the prince of this world <u>hath been judged</u>.

Next, regarding this war is, what does Satan do to try to draw men away from God? How is this accomplished, and why does he go through all of this trouble to achieve this? There must be an excellent reason for this. If we return to the epistle that the apostle Paul wrote to the church in Ephesus, we will see in chapter 2:2-3:

Wherein ye once walked according to the course of this world, according to the prince of the powers of the air, of the spirit that now worketh in the sons of disobedience; among whom we also all once lived in the lusts of our flesh, doing the desires of the flesh and of the mind, and were by nature children of wrath, even as the rest:

Words and phrases such as "walked," "worketh," and "once lived" are verbs because they show action. This relation to the kingdom of darkness is an active one, though it was indeed possible to be a member and to accomplish nothing. Surely the devil enjoys all of the evil performed by his children, though he hates every captive he possesses. Each prisoner is just another feather in his cap.

Satan has several tools that he uses to exert his power and influence over mankind. These are in diametrical opposition to God and his program. In 2 Corinthians 4:3-4 scripture says:

And even if our gospel is veiled, it is veiled in them that per-ish: in whom the god of this world hath blinded the minds of the unbelieving, that the light of the gospel of the glory of Christ, who is the image of God, should not dawn upon them.

This verse tells us a great deal about Satan's program to oppose humanity and keep us in bondage. We learn:

1. Satan is the "god" of this world.
2. He can blind the minds (meaning he has actual power) of those who are unbelieving.
3. He can keep the unsaved blind as to the plan of salvation. He can take it away.

This ought to be a great incentive to those of us who can teach, to do it thoroughly, with power, and to overcome his influence with the superior power of the gospel. Let's take a quick look at the Parable of the Sower to see him at work again stealing the words of life from the mind of a prospective believer. Matthew 13:19

When any one heareth the word of the kingdom, and under-standeth it not, then cometh the evil one, and snatcheth away that which hath been sown in his heart. This is he that was sown by the way side.

Remember, this a parable that came from the Lord's lips. This is a divine commentary on an awful situation indeed.

Next, note the principle in 2 Thessalonians 3:5:

For this cause I also, when I could no longer forbear, sent that I might know your faith, lest by any means the tempter had tempted you, and our labor should be in vain.

Paul is concerned that Satan has tempted the believers to the point where they are separated from God. Now, I need to stress that he cannot take you away against your own will, but he can so tempt you that you turn and walk away from God. This is where his power lies. Although his power is greater than ours *individually* (that is, he has greater power than any individual human), when we are walking in fellowship with the Lord, *we* have more power be-cause of the One walking with us. The great power of the Son of

God dwarfs Satan's power. I stress this again, Satan's power is higher than ours individually, but it can never overcome the power that is in Jesus Christ.

This power of our Lord is on display when Jesus did battle with Satan in the wilderness (Matthew 4:1-11). Here the struggle for our souls was fought and won by our beloved Savior. Satan tried to tempt our Lord in his weakened state, through hunger and suffering, but lost. In Jesus' victory, Satan was judged and hurled down. It was through the life of Christ that the power of Satan was crushed, just like the prophecy given by God in Genesis 3:15.

> *and I will put enmity between thee and the woman, and between thy seed and her seed: he shall bruise thy head, and thou shalt bruise his heel.*

Indeed, the head was crushed.

Another tactic of Satan's is given in John 8:44:

> *Ye are of your father, the devil, and the lusts of your father it is your will to do. He was a murderer from the beginning, and standeth not in the truth, because there is no truth in him. When he speaketh <u>a lie</u>, he speaketh of his own: for he is a liar, and the father thereof.*

Here, Jesus is addressing the Jewish religious leaders, but he is also directing his speech towards Satan. The serpent lied to our mother, Eve. The lie: *Ye shall not surely die.* By believing and acting on that lie, Adam and Eve spiritually and, eventually, physically died, hence the murder charge. Disobedience to God is sin and sin kills as surely as if it were a gun pointed at your heart. These lies, Satan's bread and butter, results in our deaths. Again, he does not have the power to overcome us against our will, but he can lead us away from God through lies and half-truths. There is power in the tongue!

> *For such men are false apostles, deceitful workers, fashioning themselves into apostles of Christ. And no marvel; for even Satan fashioneth himself into an angel of light. It is no great thing; therefore, if his ministers also fashion themselves as ministers of righteousness, whose end shall be according to their works (2 Corinthians 11:13).*

These verses have a myriad of implications in them.

1. There are false apostles. There are deceitful workers.
2. These hypocritically act.
3. Satan changes his real appearance into an angel of light.
4. His deceitful workers change their appearance as their master does.
5. They have judgment coming upon them.

The only question that we are not told of is how many skeletons will be in their closet? How many victims will there be? Only those who walk away from the saving power of Christ will be victims. Another scripture given us is:

> *Beloved, believe not every spirit, but prove the spirits, whether they are of God; because many false prophets are gone out into the world (1 John 4:1).*

We are to test the spirits that come to us. Through lies and hypocrisy, those who do not test the spirits are in danger of being led away from the saving power of the blood of Jesus Christ. Again, they cannot *drag* you away; they have to *lead* you away, so don't go anywhere if you have any doubts as to who you are with. It might seem a little over-dramatic, but your eternal salvation might just be at stake. Think on these things! (Phil. 4:8)

> *But the Spirit saith expressly, that in later times some shall fall away from the faith, giving heed to seducing spirits and doctrines of demons, through the hypocrisy of men that speak lies, branded in their own conscience as with a hot iron; forbidding to marry, and commanding to abstain from meats, which God created to be received with thanksgiving by them that believe and know the truth (1 Timothy 4:1-3).*

Here, we see something new to us: seducing spirits and doctrines of demons. These are more of Satan's weaponry against us. We must use the armor that God has given us (these will be discussed in depth later on). Provisions have been made to enable us to properly deal with every attack launched by the devil. God's word is our offensive weapon and must be used to attack our opponent whenever it is needed.

In discussing the battle that is around us, we need to realize that there is a battle which is carried on **inside** each one of us. Galatians 5:16-18 shows us the extent and duration of this civil war that we face. It tells us:

> *But I say, Walk by the Spirit, and ye shall not fulfill the lust of the flesh. For the flesh lusteth against the Spirit, and the Spirit against the flesh; for these are contrary the one to the other; that ye may not do the things that ye would. But if ye are led by the Spirit, ye are not under the law.*

To understand the verse, we need to know that the word "walk" here does not mean the "mode of ambulation." It is correctly understood as our "manner of life." Thus, it means: "If your manner of life" is according to the spirit, ye shall not fulfill the lust of the flesh. Pardon my poor translation skills, but you can understand what I am trying to say. See Galatians 5:25:

> *If we live by the Spirit, by the Spirit let us also walk.*

The previous verses tell us what the result will be if our manner of life is one way or the other. Verses 19-21 are the result of following the flesh and verses 22-23 show us what the result of living a spirit-filled life is. It behooves us to follow the spirit. This is that "civil war" spoken of earlier. One part wants to live it up while the other part wants fellowship with God. Which one will it be?

Now, to add another obstacle to living a spiritual life, let's discuss the third opponent. That is the world in which we live. It is the world, the flesh, and the devil. A triple play of misery! Why does the world stand in opposition to God? 1 John 2:15-17 tells us:

> *Love not the world, neither the things that are in the world. If any man love the world, the love of the Father is not in him. For all that is in the world, the lust of the flesh and the lust of the eyes and the vainglory of life, is not of the Father, but is of the world. And the world passeth away, and the lust thereof: but he that doeth the will of God abideth forever.*

Another scripture that helps explain the enmity of the world is James 4:2-4.

> *Ye lust, and have not: ye kill, and covet, and cannot obtain: ye fight and war; ye have not, because ye ask not. Ye ask, and re-*

ceive not, because ye ask amiss, that ye may spend it in your pleasures. Ye adulteresses, know ye not that the friendship of the world is enmity with God? Whosoever, therefore, would be a friend of the world maketh himself an enemy of God.

Why is Satan able to use this against us? 1 John 5:19 reveals that:

We know that we are of God, and the whole world lieth in the evil one.

That is why. The enemy has such a hold on the world because of the sin that is routinely committed every day. Satan's power is in sin and death, and man has no control because he is bound up in the power of sin.

For all have sinned, and fall short of the glory of God (Romans 3:23).

Romans 6:23 then tells us:

For the wages of sin is death; but the free gift of God is eternal life in Christ Jesus our Lord.

That is the explanation for why the world is the enemy of God. We all are in sin, (outside of Jesus Christ, that is) and have died because of that sin. Satan is the "god of this world" because he captured it by his defeat of our first parents. We are *in* this world and *of* it because we are dead in sin. That is why he has so much power over those who are in sin. To look at it in another way, Ephesians 2:1-2 says:

And you did he (Christ) make alive, when ye were dead through your trespasses and sins, wherein ye once walked according to the course of this world, according to the prince of the powers of the air, of the spirit that now worketh in the sons of disobedience.

Christ's victorious life gave the victory to those who obey him.

Chapter Seven:
The Inward War

Mention was made in the previous chapter that mankind is a dual being. He has a spiritual body as well as a physical body. Genesis 1:27 says:

And God created man in his image, in the image of God created he him; male and female created he them.

The spiritual creation of God (making man in his image) is man's spirit. John 4:24:

God is a Spirit: and they that worship him must worship in spirit and truth.

Our physical make-up is seen in Genesis 2:7:

And Jehovah God formed man of the dust of the ground and breathed into his nostrils the breath of life, and man became a living soul.

Ecclesiastes 12:7 tells us:

and the dust returneth to the earth as it was, and the spirit returneth unto God who gave it.

2 Corinthians 4:16:

Wherefore we faint not, but though our outward man is decaying, yet our inward man is renewed day by day.

This is absolute proof that we are dual beings. When the outer man so decays as to die physically, then the inward spirit shall return to God, who gave it.

The Scriptures make a significant distinction between the physical body and the spiritual body. Jesus tells his disciples in Matthew 10:28:

And be not afraid of them that kill the body, but are not able to kill the soul: but rather fear him who is able to destroy both soul and body in hell.

We should fear God and not mankind. And as far as those who walk in error we see:

> *to deliver such a one unto Satan for the <u>destruction of the flesh</u>, that <u>the spirit</u> may be saved in the day of the Lord Jesus (1 Corinthians 5:5).*

Being both physical AND spiritual beings, we must have some sort of relationship in each of these realms. It is easy to see and be in the physical world, as we see that every day. The question is, what sort of relationship do we have to the vast spiritual realm? Romans 8:5-9 gives a good explanation.

> *For they that are after the flesh mind the things of the flesh; but they that are after the Spirit the things of the Spirit. For the mind of the flesh is death; but the mind of the Spirit is life and peace: because the mind of the flesh is enmity against God; for it is not subject to the law of God, neither indeed can it be: and they that are in the flesh cannot please God. But ye are not in the flesh but in the Spirit if so be that the Spirit of God dwelleth in you. But if any man hath not the Spirit of Christ, he is none of his.*

Colossians 3:1-2 gives a bit more information to those who seek to know.

> *If then ye were raised together with Christ, seek the things that are above, where Christ is, seated on the right hand of God. Set your mind on the things that are above, not on the things that are upon the earth.*

We can do what the Colossian letter suggests only because we are that dual being. Next, let us look at another facet of the struggle that is within every one of us on this earth.

God created man and gave each a wonderful gift—that of free-will. We have a choice of what we want to do, and that is a tremendous gift indeed. The other option would have been not to give us free-will and be faced with a large number of robots. The freedom to choose is a wonderful gift, because it frees us from being those robots and makes us able to make a choice. On the other hand, it was also a very dangerous choice for God, as we could reject him, and turn our backs on him. The experiment had been conducted before, with the creation of the angels in heaven. Scripture tells us that they had the same choice to make, and one-third of them revolted and followed the being we know as Satan. This led to war in heaven, which was on until Jesus' victorious win on the cross. Satan's power was broken, and he was cast out of heaven.

And he said unto them, I beheld Satan fallen as lightning from heaven (Luke 10:18).

At this point, I see the value of listing some verses that can offer you more than my poor commentary.

For as he thinketh within himself, so is he: Eat and drink, saith he to thee; But his heart is not with thee (Proverbs 23:7).

Come now, and let us reason together, saith Jehovah: though your sins be as scarlet, they shall be as white as snow; though they be red like crimson, they shall be as wool. If ye be willing and obedient, ye shall eat the good of the land: but if ye refuse and rebel, ye shall be devoured with the sword; for the mouth of Jehovah hath spoken it (Isaiah 1:18-20).

And he said unto them, Unto you is given the mystery of the kingdom of God: but unto them that are without, all things are done in parables: that seeing they may see, and not perceive, and hearing they may hear, and not understand; lest haply they should turn again, and it should be forgiven them (Mark 4:11-12).

Try your own selves, whether ye are in the faith; prove your own selves. Or know ye not as to your own selves, that Jesus Christ is in you? unless indeed ye be reprobate. But I hope that ye shall know that we are not reprobate (2 Corinthians 13:5-6)

These few verses show how free-will acts. You have a choice on whether you will obey the Lord or not. Some decisions have very serious implications; it is essential that we know this and are prepared to act properly to be pleasing to God. Otherwise, the choice to reject God has the same penalty as the one the devil and his angels made. Scripture teaches that Hell was created for the devil and his angels. Disobedient men face the same future by the choices that they make every day.

Mankind can make proper choices and very often does. But there are always those who do not believe and thus make terrible decisions which have eternal implications for themselves and others. Such an example would be of someone who drinks a large amount of alcohol and then gets behind the wheel. Not only can they maim or outright kill themselves, but they destroy innocent lives of those who made right decisions.

Now, back to right decisions. Joshua 24:12-15 tells us:

> *And I sent the hornet before you, which drove them out from before you, even the two kings of the Amorites; not with thy sword, nor with thy bow. And I gave you a land whereon thou hadst not labored, and cities which ye built not, and ye dwell therein; of vineyards and oliveyards which ye planted not do ye eat. Now, therefore, fear Jehovah, and serve him in sincerity and in truth; and put away the gods which your fathers served beyond the River, and in Egypt; and serve ye Jehovah. And if it seem evil unto you to serve Jehovah, choose you this day whom ye will serve; whether the gods which your fathers served that were beyond the River, or the gods of the Amorites, in whose land ye dwell: but as for me and my house, we will serve Jehovah.*

Deuteronomy 30:19:

> *I call heaven and earth to witness against you this day, that I have set before thee life and death, the blessing and the curse: therefore choose life, that thou mayest live, thou and thy seed; to love Jehovah thy God, to obey his voice, and to cleave unto him; for he is thy life, and the length of thy days; that thou mayest dwell in the land which Jehovah sware unto thy fathers, to Abraham, to Isaac, and to Jacob, to give them.*

In each of these sections, God calls the nation of Israel to a life of obedience and fellowship with himself. They have that free-will which makes it possible to deny God, but their overall common sense (in which they were on again, off again) made them pledge to walk with and serve Jehovah. At least it happened at times. The

52

book of Judges is a wonderful example of their hot and cold relationship with God.

Our God, being a wonderful, loving God, can overlook much because of the sacrifice that Jesus made at Calvary. Our sins are paid for, though his true followers strive to avoid sin if at all possible.

Another help that God gave to us is our conscience. Properly educated, this internal compass helps pilot us through the day. An uneducated conscience can be quickly silenced by ungodly behavior. In Romans 2:13-15 we see:

for not the hearers of the law are just before God, but the doers of the law shall be justified: (for when Gentiles that have not the law do by nature the things of the law, these, not having the law, are the law unto themselves in that they show the work of the law written in their hearts, their conscience bearing witness therewith, and their thoughts one with another accusing or else excusing them);

This talks about the law of God being on their hearts and how it does its work on a daily basis. We must educate it and always keep it clean by staying out of sinful situations and avoiding the ungodly, whose vile speech can ruin anything.

having a good conscience; that, wherein ye are spoken against, they may be put to shame who revile your good manner of life in Christ (1 Peter 3:16)

The world strives to pollute holy things. If you listen to their course, vulgar speech, you can see where the pollutions come from.

Next, we see the conscience at work. See how it works in men's hearts:

And the scribes and the Pharisees bring a woman taken in adultery; and having set her in the midst, they say unto him, Teacher, this woman hath been taken in adultery, in the very act. Now in the law Moses commanded us to stone such: what then sayest thou of her? And this they said, trying him, that they might have whereof to accuse him. But Jesus stooped down, and with his finger wrote on the ground. But when they continued asking him, he lifted up himself, and said unto them, He that is without sin among you, let him first cast a stone at her. And again, he stooped down, and with his finger wrote on the ground. And they, when they heard it, went out one by one, beginning from the eldest, even unto the last: and Jesus was left alone, and the woman, where she was, in the midst (John 8:3-9).

As mentioned before, the conscience is a beautiful God-given tool that requires constant training and exercise. If there is no training provided (by God's word, for example), outright attempts to quiet or destroy this aid can occur. It can be damaged by hardening and overriding any attempts to listen to it. In 1 Timothy 4: 2 we read:

But the Spirit saith expressly, that in later times some shall fall away from the faith, giving heed to seducing spirits and doctrines of demons, through the hypocrisy of men that speak lies, branded in their own conscience as with a hot iron;

These characters sought to burn their conscience out. They did not want to hear what God had to say, as it undoubtedly was the opposite of what their intentions were. Anyone with a heart so dark will undoubtedly seek to silence any restraining force. They are self-centered and do not care to hear anyone try to set them straight. The world is full of them, and we need to be able to recognize them and stay away. In Acts 24:25, scripture says:

And as [Paul] reasoned of righteousness, and self-control, and the judgment to come, Felix was terrified, and answered, Go thy way for this time; and when I have a convenient season, I will call thee unto me. He hoped withal that money would be given him of Paul: wherefore also he sent for him the oftener and communed with him.

Felix was the governor after Festus, under who Paul was taken prisoner by his Jewish enemies. Either man could have released Paul, but neither one did. Festus wanted to give the Jews a gift while Felix sought to fill his coin box from Paul's friends by a bribe. But, it just wasn't going to happen.

There is another subject that is not at all popular among the children of men. That is our accountability to God for what we say and do. For example, Matthew 12:36:

And I say unto you, that every idle word that men shall speak, they shall give account thereof in the day of judgment.

Romans 14:12-15:

But thou, why dost thou judge thy brother? or thou again, why dost thou set at nought thy brother? for we shall all stand before the judgment-seat of God. For it is written, As I live, saith the Lord, to me every knee shall bow, And every tongue shall confess to God. So then each one of us shall give account of himself to God.

2 Corinthians 5:10-11:

For we must all be made manifest before the judgment-seat of Christ; that each one may receive the things done in the body, according to what he hath done, whether it be good or bad. Knowing, therefore, the fear of the Lord, we persuade men.

With these assurances of our responsibilities, we ought to devote a great deal more time and effort in right living and proper speech. We will give account, something like the three servants in the parable of the talents as given in Matthew 25:14-30. Those servants also had to give an account of their actions.

Now, let's return to a subject that received some coverage in an earlier chapter. That is the ongoing battle that rages inside every one of us every day. Galatians 5:16-17 sheds some light on the ongoing battle. What can we do to overcome?

But I say, Walk by the Spirit, and ye shall not fulfill the lust of the flesh. For the flesh lusteth against the Spirit, and the Spirit against the flesh; for these are contrary the one to the other; that ye may not do the things that ye would.

Romans 7:14-25

For we know that the law is spiritual: but I am carnal, sold under sin. For that which I do I know not: for not what I would, that do I practice; but what I hate, that I do. But if what I would not, that I do, I consent unto the law that it is good. So now it is no more I that do it, but sin which dwelleth in me. For I know that in me, that is, in my flesh, dwelleth no good thing: for to will is present with me, but to do that which is good is not. For the good which I would I do not: but the evil which I would not, that I practice. But if what I would not, that I do, it is no more I that do it, but sin which dwelleth in me. I find then the law, that, to me who would do good, evil is present. For I delight in the law of God after the inward man: but I see a different law in my members, warring against the law of my mind, and bringing me into captivity under the law of sin which is in my members. Wretched man that I am! who shall deliver me out of the body of this death? I thank God through Jesus Christ our Lord. So, then I of myself with the mind, indeed, serve the law of God; but with the flesh the law of sin.

This rather long section shows just how bad the struggle can be when the flesh is opposing the spirit. There is never any peace for one who has just such a conflict going on in his life. It is vital to spend time in prayer and read God's word. Perhaps you have a friend or brother who is spiritually minded. Get to them as quickly as you can. Get out of the area where the temptation is. Remember Joseph? He needed to get out so badly that he left his clothing in the woman's hand. He did avoid the sin but paid for it anyway. Do whatever you have to do!! 1 Corinthians 10 tells us that God has a way of escape if we look for it. Victory over temptation is victory over Satan, and I find that to be sweet indeed. Have the right mind-set!!

How do we achieve victory? One side will be the victor, and it is our goal to win that battle. Romans 8:6-11 says:

For the mind of the flesh is death; but the mind of the Spirit is life and peace: because the mind of the flesh is enmity against God; for it is not subject to the law of God, neither indeed can it be: and they that are in the flesh cannot please God. But ye are not in the flesh but in the Spirit, if so be that the Spirit of God dwelleth in you. But if any man hath not the Spirit of Christ, he is none of his. And if Christ is in you, the body is dead because of sin; but the spirit is life because of righteousness. But if the Spirit of him that raised up Jesus from the dead dwelleth in you, he that raised up Christ Jesus from the dead shall give life also to your mortal bodies through his Spirit that dwelleth in you.

Galatians 5:22-24:

But the fruit of the Spirit is love, joy, peace, longsuffering, kindness, goodness, faithfulness, meekness, self-control; against such, there is no law. <u>And they that are of Christ Jesus have crucified the flesh with the passions and the lusts thereof.</u>

That is how you overcome the trials and temptations which are thrown at us by the enemy and his forces. God's armor (soon to be covered) is made for just this sort of situation. Soon enough, you will have the armor and wear it with pride. This is yet another gift from our gracious Father. Prayer and fasting can also be a great source of strength. Singing gospel songs also is a big help when the temptations come upon us. Focusing on God's word and how Jesus cast every temptation down will be a great help. We must have the right mindset when we are being attacked by the enemy of our souls. Romans 12:2 says:

And be not fashioned according to this world: but be ye transformed by the renewing of your mind, that ye may prove what is the good and acceptable and perfect will of God.

We cannot maintain things as usual. We must make a change in our manner of life. Passages like 2 Corinthians 13:5 help us to look at ourselves the way that God does. Having then seen our errors, prayer and Bible study will get us into the right mind to get back to doing things in God's way. That is pleasing—when we are ready, willing, and able to make the necessary elements to be pleasing to Him!

Next, look at 2 Corinthians 10:4-6.

(for the weapons of our warfare are not of the flesh, but mighty before God to the casting down of strongholds), casting down imaginations, and every high thing that is exalted against the knowledge of God, and bringing every thought into captivity to the obedience of Christ; and being in readiness to avenge all disobedience, when your obedience shall be made full.

As I said earlier, it is so vital that we maintain the proper mind-set so that we can resist the devil and win the victory with our beloved Savior!! There can be no surrendering just because we are tired or not feeling well. The results of these contests have eternal consequences. We must have the proper mind-set and to not lose it when things get tricky! 1 Corinthians 2:14-16 tells us:

> *Now the natural man receiveth not the things of the Spirit of God: for they are foolishness unto him; and he cannot know them, because they are spiritually judged. But he that is spiritual judgeth all things, and he himself is judged of no man. For who hath known the mind of the Lord, that he should instruct him? But we have the mind of Christ.*

Having obtained that precious mind-set, we must give all diligence to maintain it. Let no one or nothing bring us down. Anger? Wrath? Let nothing stop you!!

> *But ye are not in the flesh but in the Spirit, if so be that the Spirit of God dwelleth in you. But if any man hath not the Spirit of Christ, he is none of his (Romans 8:9).*

Finally, Both God and Satan struggle for control of our minds and then lives. The battle continues until we yield to either one or the other. Trying to operate in both realms is very dangerous.

> *For let not that man think that he shall receive anything of the Lord; a doubleminded man, unstable in all his ways (James 1:7-8).*

True liberation can only come when we entirely give in to God.

> *This I say therefore, and testify in the Lord, that ye no longer walk as the Gentiles also walk, in the vanity of their mind, being darkened in their understanding, alienated from the life of God, because of the ignorance that is in them, because of the hardening of their heart; who being past feeling gave themselves up to lasciviousness, to work all uncleanness with greediness. But ye did not so learn Christ; if so be that ye heard him, and were taught in him, even as truth is in Jesus: that ye put away, as concerning your former manner of life, the old man, that waxeth corrupt after the lusts of deceit; and that ye be renewed in the spirit of your mind, and put on the*

new man, that after God hath been created in righteousness and holiness of truth (Ephesians 4:17-24).

Chapter Eight:
Our Adversary

There are so many different ideas about this being. Does he really exist? Is he real or merely a concept that is in someone's head? If you look around at some of the horrible things that so routinely happen, you know that *something* has to be behind it all. The mass killings and strange things people do "in his name" lead you to believe that there might be someone out there who has a real problem. Does that peculiar little figure with the horns and pitchfork exist? That comical figure makes you want to laugh, but then you remember some of the things he is responsible for and any laughter you had quickly disappeared. Once upon a time, there was a comedian who would say, "the devil made me do it." There is not much to laugh about any longer.

The Bible presents Satan as a genuine being that has a real agenda. His program is to oppose God at every possible turn. Let us examine the subject in light of the scriptures and avoid all of the conjecture that is often made by those of the religious world. In Matthew 4:1, we read:

> *Then was Jesus led up of the Spirit into the wilderness to be tempted of the devil.*

We see that he is, in fact, a real being and that he tempts people.

> *But when the Pharisees heard it, they said, This man doth not cast out demons, but by Beelzebub, the prince of the demons (Matthew 12:24).*

A name for the devil is Beelzebub, and he is the prince of the demons.

> *and if Satan casteth out Satan, he is divided against himself; how then shall his kingdom stand? And if I by Beelzebub cast out demons, by whom do your sons cast them out? therefore shall they be your judges (Matthew 12:25-26).*

The devil, known as Satan and Beelzebub, has a kingdom of his own.

And he said unto them, An enemy hath done this. And the servants say unto him, Wilt thou then that we go and gather them up? ...and the enemy that sowed them is the devil... (Matthew 13:28, 29).

Here, we see that he does things against others and is an enemy.

Now is the judgment of this world: now shall the prince of this world be cast out (John 12:31).

He has been judged and cast out. Your crimes have to be pretty severe to be cast out.

in whom the god of this world hath blinded the minds of the unbelieving, that the light of the gospel of the glory of Christ, who is the image of God, should not dawn upon them (2 Corinthians 4:4).

He is the god of this world, and he can steal the gospel out of your heart. This picture is getting pretty dark indeed.

wherein ye once walked according to the course of this world, according to the prince of the powers of the air, of the spirit that now worketh in the sons of disobedience (Ephesians 2:2).

He is the Prince of the Powers of the Air. He leads men in defiance.

Be sober, be watchful: your adversary the devil, as a roaring lion, walketh about, seeking whom he may devour (1 Peter 5:8).

Wow! He walks about seeking to devour men. And he is our adversary!

And the great dragon was cast down, the old serpent, he that is called the Devil and Satan, the deceiver of the whole world; he was cast down to the earth, and his angels were cast down with him (Revelation 12:9).

He is known as the great dragon, and he deceives the whole world. He and his angels were cast down to earth. That concludes a pretty frightening picture of an evil being. Going by just these few references (and there are more), I think a reasonably good image can be made. We spoke earlier of his appearing like an Angel of Light.

That is disheartening enough as it stands, but now every person who is "religious" must come under suspicion and mistrust. What an awful shame!

We know that he was involved in a war in heaven and was cast out, so we must understand that besides being *our* enemy, he is an enemy *to God*. God has created a place for him—Hell—where all who follow him will spend the remainder of eternity. I am sure that some will hope for annihilation, but that cannot happen because scripture tells us that those in Hell will be there as long as those who are in Heaven. Eternity will never end!

In John 8:44, we read:

> *Ye are of your father the devil, and the lusts of your father it is your will to do. He was a murderer from the beginning, and standeth not in the truth, because there is no truth in him. When he speaketh a lie, he speaketh of his own: for he is a liar, and the father thereof.*

He brought lies and even murder into being. His natural speech is to lie. How do they all work together if they lie to one another? That must be tremendously difficult—to which we say Bravo! In Acts 13:10, Paul is speaking to Elymas the Sorcerer, and says:

> *O full of all guile and all villany, thou son of the devil, thou enemy of all righteousness, wilt thou not cease to pervert the right ways of the Lord?*

What wrath and indignation from Paul. This fellow surely was like his master: full of guile, son of the devil, the enemy of all righteousness. Now THAT is a list of charges! Even if we just take all the notes I made here (and again, there is much more that could be said), we have a long and horrible list.

Next, I would like to take a look at his origin. I am afraid that I cannot provide the entertaining stories, as that is just what they are—stories. If we take the facts as given by Scripture, we can get a fair picture of what he is and where he came from.

First, we must ask the question; is Satan a created, or is he a divine being? Let's look at that first. Colossians 1:16 says:

> *for in him (Christ) were all things created, in the heavens and upon the earth, things visible and things invisible, whether*

thrones or dominions or principalities or powers; all things have been created through him, and unto him.

It says, in Christ were all things created, even thrones, dominions, principalities, and powers—all seen to be associated with evil in the New Testament. If he created all things, Satan—or whatever he was before he fell, was created too. There can be no comparison with God, as in good versus evil, as it would more likely be Satan versus the Archangel Michael. He may make boasts of his high standing, but the facts simply do not match up.

By looking at and analyzing the many biblical passages on the Devil, it becomes evident that he is the most powerful creature in all of God's universe. He, the most depraved and deadly being, possesses more strength and savvy than any archangel or mere saint. Our power comes from Jesus Christ and his victory at Calvary. But, in spite of this, he is still a creature and not the Creator. Because of this blessed truth, his power and knowledge are limited.

We shall now consider some of the restrictions God has placed on this terrible being.

1. **He is not omnipresent.** He cannot be in two places at once. However, this does not mean that he can't tempt two saints at the same time in different locations as he does oversee a network of myriads of demons who work to do his bidding. This network gives him increased power and intelligence.

2. **He is not omnipotent**. While he is still the possessor of the greatest strength in our physical universe, in comparison to God's immense power, he is vastly overwhelmed and outnumbered.

3. **He is not omniscient**. Having been here for the entire length of human history, he has gained an immense amount of knowledge but is ignorant of many things. He knows nothing of God's love, mercy, grace, and forgiveness. He can't tell the future nor all the secrets of the past. He surely knows the Bible well enough to know of his future fate but is likely so corrupted by sin that he even might think that it is possible to defeat God. He surely advances across the battlefield, thinking that it just might be possible still.

What did Satan do with the authority which was given to him? What will he do with it in the future? We read in Jude verse 6:

And angels that kept not their own principality, but left their proper habitation, he hath kept in everlasting bonds under darkness unto the judgment of the great day.

2 Peter 2:4, 9 adds:

For if God spared not angels when they sinned, but cast them down to hell, and committed them to pits of darkness, to be reserved unto judgment... the Lord knoweth how to deliver the godly out of temptation, and to keep the unrighteous under punishment unto the day of judgment.

It seems that these rebels are under bondage now or would most likely be causing even more trouble than they are.

The greatest trouble that Satan causes among those who follow Christ is the mischief caused by the perversion of God's word. The following is a small list of his activities.

1. He sows tares in God's wheat, using pseudo-Christians, he causes false doctrine to spread among God's children.
2. He instigates false doctrine. 1 Timothy 4:1-3 tells of false teachers coming into the church and polluting the pure word by doctrines of demons.
3. He causes misinterpretations of the word. Churches are split by false teachers and doctrines of demons.
4. He takes the word out of context. He tried to get Jesus to throw himself off of the temple (Matthew 4:6). He outright lied to Eve about "Ye shall not surely die" (Genesis 3:4).
5. He hinders the work of God's servants. See 1 Thessalonians 2:18
6. He Resists the prayers of the saints. See Daniel 10:12-13
7. Blinds men to the truth. "In whom the god of this world hath blinded the minds of them that believe not..." (2 Corinthians 4:4).
8. He steals the Word of God from human hearts. (Matthew 13:19).
9. He accuses the faithful before God. (Job 1:7-12, Revelation 12:10).

Finally, what awaits this terrible being? What does his future hold? We know that he has been judged. John 16:7-11 seals his fate. It says:

Nevertheless, I tell you the truth: It is expedient for you that I go away; for if I go not away, the Comforter will not come unto you; but if I go, I will send him unto you. And he, when he comes, will convict the world in respect of sin, and of righteousness, and of judgment: of sin, because they believe not on me; of righteousness, because I go to the Father, and ye behold me no more; of judgment, <u>because the prince of this world hath been judged.</u>

We see his end where the judgment will be carried out, and he will be cast into the lake of fire where he will be tormented day and night forever. This is found in the book of Revelation.

Chapter Nine:
The Devices of Satan

We can't just leave the topic of Satan without discussing the methods, the tools that he uses. Scripture calls them his "devices." Webster's dictionary defines a "device" as "a thing devised, planned, a scheme or trick." So, in reality, what we are looking at is the "plan" or "scheme" of Satan. That seems to fit rather well. The 2 Corinthians 2:11, says: *that no advantage may be gained over us by Satan: for we are not ignorant of his devices.*

Is his power endless like God's, or is it limited? We can see in Job 1:12:

> *And Jehovah said unto Satan, Behold, all that he hath is in thy power; only upon himself put not forth thy hand. So Satan went forth from the presence of Jehovah.*

Here, God gives Satan access to Job after his accusation that Job was faithful only because God had placed a wall around him. Later, in 2:6, Satan again asks for access to Job's person as the first test had failed. 2:6-7:

> *And Jehovah said unto Satan, Behold, he is in thy hand; only spare his life. So, Satan went forth from the presence of Jehovah, and smote Job with sore boils from the sole of his foot unto his crown.*

Job suffered terribly at Satan's hand but remained faithful and received back all that had been taken away.

In New Testament times, Satan was back at his job of spreading misery and suffering. He approaches God with the intent of trying the apostles. Except, at this time, God's answer is a definite "NO." Jesus said:

> *Simon, Simon, behold, Satan asked to have you, that he might sift you as wheat.*

He does not have the power to do these things on his own but must approach the Lord for permission to do whatever it is that he seeks to do. That should bring much relief to the saints.

It is much to our relief that God holds all of the power and delegates whatever needs to be accomplished to whoever must do so. We are not under the control of the forces of the kingdom of darkness. Jesus, in John 10:27-28, tells us:

My sheep hear my voice, and I know them, and they follow me: and I give unto them eternal life, and they shall never perish, and <u>no one shall snatch them out of my hand</u>.

1 Corinthians 10:13 is another verse which shows us God's unlimited power. It says:

There hath no temptation taken you but such as man can bear: but God is faithful, who will <u>not suffer you to be tempted above that ye are able</u>; but will with the temptation also make the way of escape, that ye may be able to endure it.

In regard to the temptation which Satan brings upon every one of us, God controls how much Satan can use on us. If it is more than you can bear, He limits it so that we will not be overcome. That is a loving God-limiting a hateful foe.

When we launch out on our own in dealing with the enemy, we would very quickly be overwhelmed if our Heavenly Father was not watching out for us. Satan's power trumps our power, and we would be swept up in a flood of evil if God were not watching over us. Thank God for Jesus...thank Jesus for God!! 1 Peter 5:8 tells us:

Be sober, be watchful: your adversary the devil, as a roaring lion, walketh about, seeking whom he may devour.

He is out there, looking for someone that he can overcome. We need to be close to our Lord and Master, who watches over us with the great loving care. He has loved us so much that he spared not his only son but sent him to die in our place! What greater love? I think that that is the greatest gift that we could ever receive!

What is the source of Satan's power and influence? From whence did it come? The first reference to Satan in the Bible is in Genesis 3:1-5:

Now the serpent was more subtle than any beast of the field which Jehovah God had made. And he said unto the woman, Yea, hath God said, Ye shall not eat of any tree of the garden?

And the woman said unto the serpent, Of the fruit of the trees of the garden we may eat: but of the fruit of the tree which is in the midst of the garden, God hath said, Ye shall not eat of it, neither shall ye touch it, lest ye die. And the serpent said unto the woman, Ye shall not surely die: for God doth know that in the day ye eat thereof, then your eyes shall be opened, and ye shall be as God, knowing good and evil.

This is where the tragedy occurred. Instead of turning to God, they listened to the serpent and partook of the fruit. They had never heard a lie before and fell for it. In this, they became dead in sin, and Satan gained power over them. John 8:44

Ye are of your father, the devil, and the lusts of your father it is your will to do. He was a murderer from the beginning, and standeth not in the truth, because there is no truth in him. When he speaketh a lie, he speaketh of his own: for he is a liar, and the father thereof.

What is Satan's domain? We know that he has some form of government because of Colossians 1:13:

who delivered us out of the <u>power of darkness</u> <u>and translated</u> us into the kingdom of the Son of his love.

What form I do not know, but it held all against their will. In what sphere is his power the greatest? 1 John 5:19 tells us:

We know that we are of God and the <u>whole world lieth in the evil one</u>.

His realm is the whole world. Imagine that. Ephesians 2:2

wherein ye once walked according to the <u>course of this world, according to the prince of the powers of the air</u>, of the spirit that now worketh in the sons of disobedience; among whom we also all once lived in the lusts of our flesh, doing the desires of the flesh and of the mind, and were by nature children of wrath, even as the rest.

We can see from the context of that last passage this world belongs to Satan in some fashion. John 12:31 says:

> *Now is the judgment of this world: now shall the prince of this world be cast out*

John 14:30:

> *I will no more speak much with you, for the prince of the world cometh: and he hath nothing in me.*

John 16:11

> *of judgment, because the prince of this world hath been judged.*

The world ruler has faced judgment and will be removed.

Satan's Transformative Tricks

After looking at the various things that Satan has done, let's look at some of his devices in dealing with the world. One of his primary devices is *to pretend to be an angel of light* rather than the prince of darkness which he is. 2 Corinthians 11:14-15 shows his main method.

> *And no marvel; for even Satan fashioneth himself into an angel of light. It is no great thing therefore if his ministers also fashion themselves as ministers of righteousness, whose end shall be according to their works.*

By appearing as holy and righteous ministers of righteousness, they can gain access and to foolish and unlearned people who have no ideas as to who these people are. Damage and discord can be accomplished in a short period. This surely has to be his most excellent work.

Some other devices include *stealing the word from the innocent and unlearned.* Luke 8:12:

> *And those by the way side are they that have heard; then cometh the devil, and taketh away the word from their heart, that they may not believe and be saved.*

Seducing spirits or doctrine of demons —what a choice! 1 Timothy 4:1:

> *But the Spirit saith expressly, that in later times some shall fall away from the faith, giving heed to seducing spirits and doctrines of demons.*

Satan is ready to s*natch away any hope that one would have in the gospel.* Gone! 2 Corinthians 4:3-4

> *And even if our gospel is veiled, it is veiled in them that perish: in whom the god of this world hath* **blinded** *the minds of the unbelieving, that the light of the gospel of the glory of Christ, who is the image of God, should not dawn upon them.*

Satan uses *lying signs and wonders* on those who do not love the truth and found pleasure in unrighteousness. 2 Thessalonians 2:9-12:

> *even he, whose coming is according to the working of Satan with all power and signs and lying wonders, and with all deceit of unrighteousness for them that perish; because they received not the love of the truth, that they might be saved. And for this cause God sendeth them a working of error, that they should believe a lie: that they all might be judged who believed not the truth but had pleasure in unrighteousness.*

Sources of Satan's Attacks

Let's take a look at where Satan's attacks come from. Matthew 7:15 is where those "ministers of righteousness" come in to play!

> *Beware of false prophets, who come to you in sheep's clothing, but inwardly are ravening wolves.*

Acts 20:29

> *I know that after my departing grievous wolves shall enter in among you, not sparing the flock; and from among your selves shall men arise, speaking perverse things, to draw away the disciples after them.*

This seems to come, one after another. Wolves are tearing up the flock, false shepherds not protecting them. Then, to top it all, members of the congregation start being puffed up, saying all sorts of things!! What a mess! Then, to top it all: 2 Peter. 2:1-3

But there arose false prophets also among the people, as among you also there shall be false teachers, who shall privily bring in destructive heresies, denying even the Master that bought them, bringing upon themselves swift destruction. And many shall follow their lascivious doings; because of whom, the way of the truth shall be evil spoken of. And in covetousness shall they with feigned words make merchandise of you: whose sentence now from of old lingereth not, and their destruction slumbereth not.

And finally, Jude 4

For there are certain men crept in privily, even they who were of old written of beforehand unto this condemnation, ungodly men, turning the grace of our God into lasciviousness, and denying our only Master and Lord, Jesus Christ.

This completes the attack. If you have survived one strike, you have done well. Virtually no one can escape them all.

The war is between God and Satan for the souls of mankind. Who do we want to serve—him who genuinely loves us or him who tries to destroy us at every turn? You be the judge!

Names of Satan

After looking at several chapters, we have seen Satan referred to by many names. Perhaps it would be a good thing to list some of these as there are many:

1. Satan (adversary) This is used some fifty-two times
2. The devil (slanderer) used thirty-five times
3. The god of this age (2 Cor. 4:4)
4. The prince of the powers of the air (Eph. 2:2)
5. The king of death (Heb. 2:14)
6. The prince of this world (Jn. 12:31)
7. The ruler of darkness (Eph. 6:12)
8. The dragon (Rev. 12:7)
9. The deceiver (Rev. 20:20)
10. Apollyon (destroyer) (Rev. 9:11)
11. Beelzebub (prince of demons) (Mt. 12:24)
12. Belial (vileness, ruthlessness) (2 Cor. 6:15)
13. The wicked one (Mt. 13:38)

14. The tempter (1 Thess. 3:5)
15. The accuser of the brethren (Rev. 12:10)
16. A false angel of light (2 Cor. 11:14-15)
17. The enemy (Mt. 13:39)
18. A roaring lion (1 Pet. 5:8)

In 2 Cor. 4:4 He uses his power of deception to control the minds of men to motivate and manipulate their actions. This is one area where he shines as a deceiver. Eph. 2:1-2

> *And you did he make alive, when ye were dead through your trespasses and sins, wherein ye once walked according to the course of this world, according to the prince of the powers of the air, of the spirit that now worketh in the sons of disobedience; among whom we also all once lived in the lusts of our flesh, doing the desires of the flesh and of the mind, and were by nature children of wrath, even as the rest.*

The world-wide and age-long works of Satan are to be traced to one predominant motive. He hates both God and man and does everything that he can to defeat God's plan of grace and to establish and maintain a kingdom of evil, in the seduction and ruin of mankind. Man is a particular victim and is eagerly sought out by his agents at every opportunity. He almost delights in his attempts to capture and ruin those who, through sin, have become his captives. This program began in the Garden of Eden with our first parents and continues even to this day. When something works as well as this does, why go through the time and trouble to replace it with something new and unproven? The old ways are the best.

Despite the antiquity of Satan's efforts to trap and destroy mankind, he goes through great efforts to make each play appear as if it were "new," "fresh," "innovative" and of course, "cutting edge." There truly is:

> *That which hath been is that which shall be; and that which hath been done is that which shall be done: and there is <u>no new thing</u> under the sun. Ecc 1:9*

Chapter Ten:
The God of This Age

It is a common error by those who know about Satan that they ascribe to him all the attributes that they do for God. This error gives him power that he usually wouldn't have. He is not a "negative image" of God. He is a very high-ranking angel that led a rebellion in heaven against God and his government. Satan is not divine, but how can he be considered *"the god of this age?"*

2 Corinthians 4:3-4:

And even if our gospel is veiled, it is veiled in them that perish: in whom the god of this world hath blinded the minds of the unbelieving, that the light of the gospel of the glory of Christ, who is the image of God, should not dawn upon them.

Also 1 John 5:18-19 says:

We know that whosoever is begotten of God sinneth not, but he that was begotten of God keepeth himself, and the evil one toucheth him not. We know that we are of God and the whole world lieth in the evil one.

The evil one has control of the entire world system. He controls the corruption, graft, and unrighteousness that occurs all over this world.

Eph. 2:1-2.

And you did he make alive, when ye were dead through your trespasses and sins, wherein ye once walked according to the course of this world, according to the prince of the powers of the air, of the spirit that now worketh in the sons of disobedience

We can see in these verses that God does something for us while we are still in sin. This is: He makes us alive. We are spiritually dead because of our sins, but if we respond to his gracious invitation, he makes us alive. We were dead, but like his son, He makes us live. Can the god of this world do that?

But, if we refuse his offer, he leaves us to do what we want. Romans 1:18-25:

> *For the wrath of God is revealed from heaven against all un-*
> *godliness and unrighteousness of men, who hinder the truth in*
> *unrighteousness; because that which is known of God is mani-*
> *fest in them; for God manifested it unto them. For the invisible*
> *things of him since the creation of the world are clearly seen,*
> *being perceived through the things that are made, even his ev-*
> *erlasting power and divinity; that they may be without excuse:*
> *because that, knowing God, they glorified him not as God,*
> *neither gave thanks; but became vain in their reasonings, and*
> *their senseless heart was darkened. Professing themselves to*
> *be wise, they became fools and changed the glory of the incor-*
> *ruptible God for the likeness of an image of corruptible man,*
> *and birds, and four-footed beasts, and creeping things.*
> *Wherefore God gave them up in the lusts of their hearts unto*
> *uncleanness, that their bodies should be dishonored among*
> *themselves: for that, they exchanged the truth of God for a lie*
> *and worshipped and served the creature rather than the Crea-*
> *tor, who is blessed for ever. Amen.*

To put in the finish to it, I turn to 1 Cor. 21-25:

> *For seeing that in the wisdom of God the world through its*
> *wisdom knew not God, it was God's good pleasure through the*
> *foolishness of the preaching to save them that believe. Seeing*
> *that Jews ask for signs, and Greeks seek after wisdom: but we*
> *preach Christ crucified, unto Jews a stumblingblock, and unto*
> *Gentiles foolishness; but unto them that are called, both Jews*
> *and Greeks, Christ the power of God, and the wisdom of God.*
> *Because the foolishness of God is wiser than men, and the*
> *weakness of God is stronger than men.*

When people make this choice, they openly reject God and lose the contact that they need to live. Rejecting the deep things of God (1 Corinthians 2:9-14) and instead go to the "deep" things that are from their master, Satan. 2 Peter 2:18-19 says:

> *For, uttering great swelling words of vanity, they entice in the*
> *lusts of the flesh, by lasciviousness, those who are just escap-*

ing from them that live in error; promising them liberty, while they themselves are bondservants of corruption; for of whom a man is overcome, of the same is he also brought into bondage. Jude 16: These are murmurers, complainers, walking after their lusts (and their mouth speaketh great swelling words), showing respect of persons for the sake of advantage.

This is what happens to those who reject God's gracious offer of life. These are the DEEP things of Satan!

When in bondage, we see things so much different than when we are made free in Christ. Some of the things which affect those in bondage are:

Religion—What is their faith like, if anything at all? They seek entertainment in "worship" with such things as "praise bands" and other similar items. Worship at the "church of your choice."

Homosexuality—They don't see it as a problem; it is more of a choice which each person makes (see Romans 1:18-25).

Moral absolutes—There are no absolutes; each man does what is right in his own eyes (Judges 17:6).

Pursuit of self—That is each man's own decision. Life is meant for enjoyment. There is no one to answer to so enjoy!

Lack of accountability—to people of the world, there is no accountability at all, marriages fail, children are born out of wedlock, and the list can go on and on.

Where these philosophies raise their heads, there is nothing but anguish and suffering. This world is so severely out-of-whack that it would take nothing less than the return of the Lord and His righteous judgment to straighten it all out. In all of this horrible mess, Satan has been very effective in hiding the truth from his prisoners. How much is known about the truth? How many people seek that truth? Enough said.

Chapter Eleven:
The Power of Temptation

We come at last to the point where we come face to face with Satan. We desire to do right while he wishes to crush and destroy us. Yes, it is that bad. He truly wants nothing short of our deaths-both physical and eternal.

The temptation is where his power lies when it comes to the Christian. He has no control over us except what we give him. That comes in the form of temptations. I use the plural in the above sentence because depending upon the person; there are lots of those!

The Bible has a lot to say on the subject. To see the best information on temptation, we turn to the book of James. James has been referred to as the "Proverbs of the New Testament" because it covers so many different topics. The best possible information can be found there. James 1:12-16

> *Blessed is the man that endureth temptation; for when he hath been approved, he shall receive the crown of life, which the Lord promised to them that love him. Let no man say when he is tempted, I am tempted of God; for God cannot be tempted with evil, and he himself tempteth no man: but each man is tempted, when he is drawn away by his own lust, and enticed. Then the lust, when it hath conceived, beareth sin: and the sin, when it is full-grown, bringeth forth death. Be not deceived, my beloved brethren.*

So much material that needs to be covered!

In verse 12, we see that God has a reward for those who overcome temptation. Verse 13 tells us unequivocally that it is not God; again, let me repeat that: It IS NOT GOD who is tempting you! *Attract*-ions are evil things in that they often lead us into sin. The temptation alone by itself is not anything at all. It is when we latch onto it that it becomes evil in that we sin by falling to the temptation. EACH MAN is tempted when his desires-referred to as" his lust" cause him to fall. That is sin and sin fully repaid causeth our death in that we are eternally separated from God. James then tells us not to be deceived-meaning, someone is trying to deceive us, and you can only imagine who that might be.

A good illustration is used from fishing, of all things. We use bait—something that looks good to a fish. It in its way lusts after that bait and goes after the bait is then caught.

Returning to our original line of thought, we need to realize that temptation happens to everyone. There are no exemptions. Even Jesus was tempted. He went without food for forty days, and then the devil came to tempt him: Matt. 4:1-11

> *Then was Jesus led up of the Spirit into the wilderness to be tempted of the devil. And when he had fasted forty days and forty nights, he afterward hungered. And the tempter came and said unto him, If thou art the Son of God, command that these stones become bread. But he answered and said, It is written, Man shall not live by bread alone, but by every word that proceedeth out of the mouth of God. Then the devil taketh him into the holy city; and he set him on the pinnacle of the temple, and saith unto him, If thou art the Son of God, cast thyself down: for it is written, He shall give his angels charge concerning thee: and, On their hands they shall bear thee up, Lest haply thou dash thy foot against a stone. Jesus said unto him, Again it is written, Thou shalt not make trial of the Lord thy God. Again, the devil taketh him unto an exceeding high mountain, and showeth him all the kingdoms of the world, and the glory of them; and he said unto him, All these things will I give thee if thou wilt fall down and worship me. Then saith Jesus unto him, Get thee hence, Satan: for it is written, Thou shalt worship the Lord thy God, and him only shalt thou serve. Then the devil leaveth him, and behold, angels came and ministered unto him.*

This ought to be the best example showing that no one was exempt from temptation!!

Having looked at these two sections of scripture, it might be suitable for use to look at how they apply.

What is the nature of some of the temptations Satan brings against us?

1 John 2:15-17—

Love not the world, neither the things that are in the world. If any man love the world, the love of the Father is not in him. For all that is in the world, the lust of the flesh and the lust of the eyes and the vainglory of life, is not of the Father, but is of the world. And the world passeth away, and the lust thereof: but he that doeth the will of God abideth forever.

In verse 16, we learn something significant to our spiritual lives. There are three main things that we must face and MUST defeat. They are

1) **The lust of the flesh** (our own tendencies being used against us-the example from fishing?)
2) **The lust of the eyes**—things are going to look good to us.
3) **The pride of life**-we are going to want to lift ourselves up in the world. Pride goeth before destruction and a haughty spirit before a fall. (Proverbs 16:18)

1 Timothy 6:9-10—

But they that are minded to be rich fall into a temptation and a snare and many foolish and hurtful lusts, such as drown men in destruction and perdition. For the love of money is a root of all kinds of evil: which some reaching after have been led astray from the faith, and have pierced themselves through with many sorrows.

Notice, it doesn't say ALL evil as an earlier translation calls, but all KINDS of evil. That is very different. Let us then remember and guard our hearts against the love of money!

Next: Matthew 13:22

And he that was sown among the thorns, this is he that heareth the word; and the care of the world, and the deceitfulness of riches, chokes the word, and he becometh unfruitful.

Another wonderful example. We can learn something. It is possible for us to let the trials and tribulations on life choke the spirituality right out of us! This is a warning from the Lord's own lips too! How much more severe can the warning be? The Judge himself has warned us about how dangerous our path can be. Let us heed His advice!

We turn to the Sermon on the Mount to learn about the next type of temptation: Matthew 5:27-28-

> *Ye have heard that it was said, Thou shalt not commit adultery: but I say unto you, that every one that <u>looketh on a woman to lust after her</u> hath <u>committed adultery</u> with her already in his heart.*

Sexual sins are one of Satan's greatest "breadwinners" He uses these in so many cases. Let us look at it closely, with a willing and seeking heart. Adultery is wrong, no question about it, but there is something even worse than the physical act, and that is thinking about it in your mind. No woman would know or willingly commit this sin, but what you think in your heart and soul is even worse in the sight of God. That is a temptation that you took hold on and, like the fish, swallowed it hook, line and sinker!! The important thing is that this is not just for men, but for women too. Also, the same principle applies in a lot of different ways. An example: you want something that you can't have. Your meditation on owning or even just having that item can be theft or at the least, idolatry—depending on how you deal with it. Sin is at the door in many situations but God is faithful who is with you. 1 Corinthians 10:12-14 will answer this problem.

> *There hath no temptation taken you but such as man can bear: but God is faithful, who will not suffer you to be tempted above that ye are able; but will with the temptation make also the way of escape, that ye may be able to endure it. Wherefore, my beloved, flee from idolatry.*

That is a wonderful breath of fresh air. It is one of those blessings that God sends to us all.

James 1:17-

> *Every good gift and every perfect gift is from above, coming down from the Father of lights, with whom can be no variation, neither shadow that is cast by turning.*

So, Satan gives you temptations; God gives you every good thing. Any comparison?

We turn to 2 Timothy 2:22 to see:

But flee youthful lusts, and follow after righteousness, faith, love, peace, with them that call on the Lord out of a pure heart.

What are youthful lusts? Are they different from the passions of other people? Well, looking with the eye of faith, we have to accept the word as it is given to us. Must youthful lusts be severe for the word to address it? Surely, it must. We are to flee them and to pursue righteousness. That is the answer, put your mind on justice, good things, holy things. In this, the Spirit will surely assist us to shun evil behavior and instead follow the paths of righteousness which lead away from such sinful behavior.

In this section, Paul speaks about his situation and how he dealt with his tormentors. 2 Corinthians 12:7-9

And by reason of the exceeding greatness of the revelations, that I should not be exalted overmuch, there was given to me a thorn in the flesh, a messenger of Satan to buffet me, that I should not be exalted overmuch. Concerning this thing, I besought the Lord thrice, that it might depart from me. And he hath said unto me, My grace is sufficient for thee: for my power is made perfect in weakness. Most gladly, therefore, will I rather glory in my infirmities, that the power of Christ may rest upon me.

He suffered greatly, but he was willing to share his situation. The lesson for us is manifold. 1) We mustn't think overly about ourselves in comparison to others but to be humble. 2) God's grace is sufficient for us, no matter what situation we might find ourselves in. Take it to him, and he'll take care of you.

Now, knowing the source of our temptations, how do we go about defeating them? Proverbs 4:23 tells us:

Keep thy heart with all diligence; For out of it are the issues of life.

Our heart is where the issues of our life begin, so that is the spot where we must defend. It is here that Satan launches His attacks and tries to get sin into our lives. Remember, God doesn't tempt us-James 1:14-15 but desires that we overcome and receive his reward.

1 Cor. 10:13

There hath no temptation taken you but such as man can bear: but God is faithful, who <u>will not</u> suffer you to be tempted above that ye are able; but will with the temptation make also the way of escape, that ye may be able to endure it.

Furthermore, Jesus is ready and willing to come to our assistance. He tells us in Hebrews 2:17-18:

Wherefore it behooved him in all things to be made like unto his brethren, that he might become a merciful and faithful high priest in things pertaining to God, to make propitiation for the sins of the people. For in that he himself hath suffered being tempted, he is able to succor them that are tempted.

4:15-16 also tells us:

For we have not a high priest that cannot be touched with the feeling of our infirmities; but one that hath been in all points tempted like as we are, yet without sin. Let us, therefore, draw near with boldness unto the throne of grace, that we may receive mercy, and may find grace to help us in time of need.

You see, temptation, like physical exercise, is necessary to growth, and God has given to us all the necessary tools that are needful to our situation. We can overcome these trials and grow stronger and mature as spiritual and physical beings.

What benefits can we hope to see as we overcome temptation every day? 1 Peter 1:5-7:

who by the power of God are guarded through faith unto a salvation ready to be revealed in the last time. Wherein ye greatly rejoice, though now for a little while, if need be, ye have been put to grief in manifold trials, that the proof of your faith, being more precious than gold that perisheth though it is proved by fire, may be found unto praise and glory and honor at the revelation of Jesus Christ.

We also see in James 1:12 that

Blessed is the man that endureth temptation; for when he hath been approved, he shall receive the crown of life, which the Lord promised to them that love him.

81

We receive promises from God who cannot lie that he will bless those who overcome and in those promises, we should find rest and reassurance to our embattled souls.

In conclusion: temptation is universal but individual as it is especially designed for every one of us, drawing upon our desires and wishes. At least the author of temptation is limited in his temptations so that we can overcome it. Our God is faithful to us and will help us through the hardships that we face. And with that, we must be grateful.

Chapter Twelve:
Learning to Say No to Ourselves—
The Power of Sin

Of all the topics to write on when writing in regards to resisting Satan, this is one of the most difficult because everything that can be said hits very close to home. "I" is the most used word in the English language. Words like "self" "me" and "mine" are high on that list as well. So, of course, when talking about sin, it does not take too long in looking at God's Word that you see that sin is a very selfish choice. Looking at James 1:14-15, we see:

> *but each man is tempted, when he is drawn away by his <u>own lust</u>, and enticed. Then the lust, when it hath conceived, beareth sin: and the sin, when it is fullgrown, bringeth forth death.*

The short term "own lust" strikes very, very close to home. Something that "we want" comes to mind. Our illustration of fishing comes to mind again—something "we want" is put in front of us, and we go after it.

Just like the instance with the fish. It sees that bait and has to go after it. To show this principle in action, let's turn to Luke 15:12-29. It is too big a reference to print out, but sections will be brought forth to show what principles are being addressed. Luke 15:11-32 is the entire section. In it, a young man (selfishly) asks for his share of the inheritance early that he may go "see the sights" a.k.a. live as he wants. The father agrees to this and gives him as he requested. He then takes this money and riotously lives, of course, spending all his money and the friends that come only with such money. Well, it happened, he woke up alone and broke. How many of us have learned that hard lesson! When money goes, then goes the friends that money brings. Who did the prodigal son care about? In Luke 15:13, we can see:

> *and the younger of them said to his father, Father, give me the portion of thy substance that falleth to me. And he divided un-*

to them his living. And not many days after, the younger son gathered all together and took his journey into a far country; and there he wasted his substance with riotous living. And when he had spent all, there arose a mighty famine in that country; and he began to be in want.

The prodigal son, in effect, cared about himself only, and he began to suffer because of it. Now, there is another one who needs consideration in this story. He also required compassion because he was bound with the bonds of self as well. We can see in Luke 15:29-31:

But he answered and said to his father, Lo, these many years do I serve thee, and I never transgressed a commandment of thine; and yet thou never gavest me a kid, that I might make merry with my friends: but when this thy son came, who hath devoured thy living with harlots, thou killedst for him the fatted calf.

We also see the "woe is me" in this story too well. This was that story all laid out with what our response should be to this character. It certainly raises the bar—that God looks out hoping for our return and repentance just like the father in this story. He was ready, willing, and able to forgive and receive him back. I think that the forgiveness which is extended to each of us will be the reason for "weeping and gnashing of teeth" when each one realizes that forgiveness was offered and they did not take it.

Self should not rank high in regards to our value as opposed to the value of another. We see in Matthew 22:36-40:

Teacher, which is the great commandment in the law? And he said unto him, Thou shalt love the Lord thy God with all thy heart, and with all thy soul, and with all thy mind. This is the great and first commandment. And a second like unto it is this, Thou shalt love thy neighbor as thyself.

Philippians 2:3-4:

On these two commandments the whole law hangeth, and the prophets doing nothing through faction or vainglory, but in lowliness of mind each counting other better than himself; not looking each of you to his own things, but each of you also to the things of others.

These two sets of verses help us to see God first and others second. I try to remember it this way: **JOY**: **J**esus first, **O**thers second and **Y**ourself last.

Since self seems to be such a threat to this divinely sponsored arrangement, what steps can we take to do something about it? Luke 9:23 says:

And he said unto all, If any man would come after me, let him <u>deny himself</u>, and take up his cross daily, and follow me.

Next: Luke 14:33

So therefore; whosoever he be of you that <u>renounceth</u> not <u>all that he hath,</u> he cannot be my disciple.

That is extra hard in this current society where goods are greatly valued.

Philippians 3:7-8

Howbeit what things were gain to me, these have I counted loss for Christ. Yea verily, and I count all things to be loss for the excellency of the knowledge of Christ Jesus my Lord: for whom I suffered the loss of all things, and do count them but refuse, that I may gain Christ, <u>I count as loss.</u> I have been crucified with Christ; and it is no longer I that live, but Christ liveth in me: and that life which I now live in the flesh I live in faith, the faith which is in the Son of God, who loved me, and gave himself up for me.

1 Corinthians 15:31

I protest by that glorying in you, brethren, which I have in Christ Jesus our Lord, I die daily. <u>I die daily.</u>

All these verses tell us that there is most definitely a way that we can deny this selfish tendency that we all have in us. This is "The Flesh" as when we spoke about our three enemies: The world, the flesh, and the devil. This is the divine prescription for our spiritual ailments. Let us have enough common sense to take the medication for us.

Some people today claim to have no control over themselves and their sinful actions—they claim to be "born this way" or seek some biological reason for their actions. We know otherwise. God has said that these things can be controlled and God does not lie.

We must take accountability for our sins. God demands it. In Psalm 51:1-4, we see:

> *Have mercy upon me, O God, according to thy lovingkind-*
> *ness: According to the multitude of thy tender mercies blot out*
> *my transgressions. Wash me thoroughly from mine iniquity,*
> *And cleanse me from my sin. For I know my transgressions;*
> *And my sin is ever before me. Against thee, thee only, have I*
> *sinned, And done that which is evil in thy sight; That thou*
> *mayest be justified when thou speakest, And be clear when*
> *thou judgest.*

We must, each and every one, take our sins to God where they can be dealt with. He has made provision for dealing with sins and will do so if we approach him with a right heart—the heart that was seen in the 51st Psalm. We seek cleansing with a sincere, honest, and willing heart. As he has shown, God is ready willing and able to do that.

How can we control or manage these selfish desires? Well, several scriptures come to mind. The first has already been stated but is important enough to repeat: Luke 9:23,

> *And he said unto all, If any man would come after me, let him*
> *deny himself, and take up his cross daily, and follow me.*

We have to deny ourselves and follow him. He will care for us, so we need not be concerned. This has to happen daily, not occasionally but daily. Next: Luke 14:33,

> *therefore, whosoever he be of you that renounceth, not all that*
> *he hath, he cannot be my disciple.*

To put physical things away. Follow him and cast off these unfruitful things which will pull you down. Follow Jesus no matter where you are, and with whatever will keep you close to him.

> *Howbeit what things were gain to me, these have I counted*
> *loss for Christ. Yea verily, and I count all things to be loss for*
> *the excellency of the knowledge of Christ Jesus my Lord: for*

whom I suffered the loss of all things, and do count them but refuse, that I may gain Christ, and be found in him, not having a righteousness of mine own, even that which is of the law, but that which is through faith in Christ, the righteousness which is from God by faith (Philippians 3:7-9).

I protest by that glorying in you, brethren, which I have in Christ Jesus our Lord, I die daily (1 Cor. 15:31).

These scriptures give us some excellent guidance and are very clear in what they are saying. We should give the more earnest heed to what they are saying to us. When God is speaking, we should be listening to Him. The reason for this insistence is because God has appointed a day in which he will judge every one of us, and that is an appointment that we have to keep. In Romans 1:18-21 we can see*:*

For the wrath of God is revealed from heaven against all ungodliness and unrighteousness of men, who hinder the truth in unrighteousness; because that which is known of God is manifest in them; for God manifested it unto them. For the invisible things of him since the creation of the world are clearly seen, being perceived through the things that are made, even his everlasting power and divinity; that they may be without excuse: because that, knowing God, they glorified him not as God, neither gave thanks; but became vain in their reasonings, and their senseless heart was darkened.

Don't let this happen to you. Pay attention to what has been said and do what needs to be done.

CONCLUSION—

"Denying oneself is not a matter of giving up something... it is a certain saying 'No' to oneself, to one's hopes and plans and ambitions, to one's likes and dislikes, to one's nearest a dearest, for the sake of Christ" (F.F. Bruce, *Hard Sayings Of Jesus*, p.152).

In a generation which is enamored with self, subduing and controlling ourselves is an even more significant challenge. But if we do not control "self," then we lose the battle to Satan.

Chapter Thirteen:
Abstain from Every Form of Evil

One lesson that each of us should learn and learn quite early is that evil comes in a great many forms. Throughout the world, it can be seen in many shapes and forms. What may be popular in one part isn't in another. God's word talks about this in 1 John 2:15:

> *Love not the world; neither the things that are in the world. If any man loves the world, the love of the Father is not in him. For all that is in the world, the lust of the flesh and the lust of the eyes and the vainglory of life, is not of the Father, but is of the world.*

Those are the three forms of our opponent The World, the Flesh and the Devil. These three work together to destroy the word of God at work in each of us. This is similar to the parable of the soils as we have given them before. Since we are looking at various forms of evil in relation to each of us, we'll next look in depth at Galatians 5:19-21 in the works of the flesh.

> *Now the <u>works of the flesh</u> are manifest, which are these: fornication, uncleanness, lasciviousness, idolatry, sorcery, enmities, strife, jealousies, wraths, factions, divisions, parties, envyings, drunkenness, revellings, and such like; of which I forewarn you, even as I did forewarn you, that they who practice such things shall not inherit the kingdom of God..*

Each one deserves a look:
   Fornication—illicit sexual intercourse
   Uncleaness—negative as far as purity
   Lasciviousness—absence of restraint, indecency
   Idolatry—slave to depraved ideas his idols represent
   Sorcery—use of medicines and drugs, witchcraft
   Enmities—opposite of agape.
   Strife—expression of enmities, contention.
   Jealousies—seek or desire eagerly(negatively)
   Wraths—hot anger, or passion.

Factions—ambition, self-seeking, rivalry
Divisions—to take asunder.
Parties—to form separately
Envyings—displeasure at hearing (good) of others-
Drunkenness—to be drunken with wine.
Revellings—consequences of drunkenness.[2]

Sin comes in many shapes and forms. In fact, as many different types as God has given us blessings. In reality, what sin is, is anything that God has given us with just a little twist to it. As an example, God has given us the physical relationship to be enjoyed among those who are married. What Satan does is to take something good and wholesome and either add to it or take from it to create sin. If you take God's wholesome marital relationship and put it outside of the marriage bed and you have fornication, which is a sin. Another item would be our need to consume food for energy. Well, if you warp that one, it becomes gluttony, which is a sin. How about prayer—something good—but if you add to it vain repetitions and strange words, you have heathen prayers which are just sounds and mean nothing. Do I need to go on? I think not because when you look at it in this light, it is easy to see.

So, after looking at the situation through the lens of God's word, we can see that each of these sins come from the desire to fulfill the lusts (appetites) of the flesh. This, of course, is at the bidding of our old opponent, Satan, and the world system that he has set up for us. We can see in 2 Peter 1:4 that

whereby he hath granted unto us his precious and exceeding great promises; that through these ye may become partakers of the divine nature, having escaped from the corruption that is in the world by lust.

Since we now know these things, we can start to deal with the desires that each of us has and to take away the power that Satan tries to exercise over us. Remember, he has no control over us except what we give him. Don't empower him by giving in to appetites, which we all naturally have.

---

[2] Definitions from Vine's Expository Dictionary.

We are to avoid and abstain from every type of evil, hating even the appearance of sin, which would stain our righteous garments (Jude 23). The lust for worldly things comes in different forms, but they all draw us away from God. Therefore, we must *"Abhor that which is evil. Cling to what is good."* (Romans 12:9).

Because this topic is so very vital to our spiritual well-being and very life, we will take a look at some Biblical failures and successes.

Failure 1—Cain 1 Jn. 3:12, 15

not as Cain was of the evil one and slew his brother. And wherefore slew he him? Because his works were evil, and his brother's righteous… Whosoever hateth his brother is a murderer: and ye know that no murderer hath eternal life abiding in him.

The entire story of Cain can be found in Genesis 4:1-24. It is too long to print out, but a few of the main points are:

4:6-7 Cain and Abel bring their offerings to God. Abel's was accepted, and Cain's was not, leading to a bad attitude. And Jehovah said unto Cain, Why art thou wroth? and why is thy countenance fallen? If thou doest well, shall it not be lifted up? and if thou doest not well, sin coucheth at the door; and unto thee shall be its desire; but do thou rule over it. It gets worse, of course, and it ends up with Abel's death. Then comes the saying of the age when God asks about his brother—verse nine says: And he said, I know not: am I my brother's keeper? Well, yes, you are. The whole incident ended with God's condemnation and his banishment. Now, that couldn't have happened better, could it?

Figure 2—Judas Iscariot—John 13:2

And during supper, the devil having already put into the heart of Judas Iscariot, Simon's son, to betray him

Without going into lengthy explanations and scriptures to prove that Jesus did not make a mistake in selecting Judas as some would imply. Jesus was deity, and deity does not make mistakes. This is from the same source of them that claim Jesus erred in his crucifixion. The best answer regarding Judas is to understand that he had his purpose, and he did it well what the exact purpose can only be left unto God, who planned the whole scenario. It was done in perfection as well as holiness.

Judas allowed Satan to have access to his heart—he gave Satan the power over himself to do whatever he (Satan) willed to do. Little did he know where that would lead. His sin was greed and he "fed it" often, culminating with the thirty pieces of silver that finished his career of wickedness. He got his just desserts.

Figure 3—Ananias and Sapphira Acts 5:1-10. This is a sad story that should never have happened, but it did. Among other things, it serves to show that temptations come to all and they have the freedom to fall. Even after they have obeyed the gospel and been washed in the blood of the Lamb, beware!! The two named people decide to sell some property and keep back some of the money and lie to everyone about how much they gave. They lied to the Holy Spirit, and it cost them their lives. Let us take heed to this solemn warning!!

Success 1—Job After the three examples of wickedness, we have an opportunity to show some examples of success.

We all know the story of Job. How he was righteous, wealthy, and had a large family. In Job 1, we see Satan pushing God to act against Job and God, allowing it under exceptional circumstances. In one day, Job lost his children and his wealth. He kept his righteousness, and Satan pushed him further, taking his health next. Even Job's wife told him to curse God and die—which, of course, he would not do. His faith indeed suffered but ultimately was upheld by trust in God, leaving Satan to slink away from the scene of the battle. God and Job were the victors. God then gave Job back his wealth and more children as well. Victory!!

Success 2—Peter We know that Peter was put to the test in a similar as Judas, but with long term success, Peter did initially fail, as did Job amid his trials but both came around and ultimately were victorious as they repented and turned back to God. Peter had denied Jesus three times in one night. When Jesus was raised, Peter repented and again returned to the service of God, ultimately gaining victory over the situation and glorifying God. We so desperately need these examples of failure as a warning to remain faithful, but we especially need to see that victory can be gained by following the standards of success. Our most excellent example is Jesus Christ himself.

Success 3—**Jesus.** Jesus was led into the wilderness and suffered terribly in being tempted to his face by Satan. This was ten times worse than temptation at a distance. He met his foe face to face and withstood every possible dart that could be sent. Hebrews 4:15 tells us:

> *For we have not a high priest that cannot be touched with the feeling of our infirmities; but one that hath been in all points tempted like as we are, yet without sin.*

He is our example to follow in every temptation that might be hurled at us. In Matthew 4:3-9, we have the case of how Satan tempted him with the world; the flesh and Jesus did not slip or even falter. We need that more than ever as time passes.

The difference between the temptations of Jesus and those of Job and Peter was that the latter two failed before they ever succeeded. Therefore, there is hope for all of us who are sinners Romans 3:23. Through faith, we can overcome!!

Chapter Fourteen:
Drawing the Line

Having looked at those examples of failure and success, we would be remiss if we forgot to talk about morality. Who determines what is moral or what is not? Let's look at the word to find out what God says is moral or not.

What is the problem with having our environment determine morals? Well, Satan controls the world system, and our flesh does not help at all. They are all under sin, so how can they give anything but evil? They can't Jeremiah 10:23 says

> *O Jehovah, I know that the way of man is not in himself: it is not in man that walketh to direct his steps.*

We can't guide ourselves and reach God's righteousness. God's will is clear concerning those actions or activities which are good or evil. We need to take heed!

Is the Bible clear about every situation in life? Is everything in the Bible "black and white" or are there some "gray areas" that we must struggle with? Does that mean that there is nothing in the Bible that is "black and white"?

When certain activities are not explicitly described in the Bible, how do we determine where to draw the line? What principles do we need to consider? God's word has the answers. Remember where it tells us all that we need for life and godliness? See 2 Peter 1:3

> *seeing that his divine power hath granted unto us all things that pertain unto life and godliness, through the knowledge of him that called us by his own glory and virtue.*

There are some principles that we can follow in guiding us in the right path.:

1) Does it destroy your identity as a Christian by causing you to be regarded as of the world (2 Corinthians 6:14; 7:1; Romans 12:1-2)?

2) Is the practice questionable in your mind and therefore, an offense to your conscience (Romans 14:23)?

3) Does it have a weakening influence on others and will it become a stumbling block to them (1 Corinthians 10:23-33; 8:7-13)?
4) Is it destructive to your body (1 Corinthians 6:19-20; 10:31)?
5) Does it conflict with your duty as a Christian (Matthew 6:33; 2 Timothy 2:4)?
6) Does it cultivate an inordinate fleshly appetite (Romans 13:13-14; 1 Corinthians 9:27)?
7) Does it bring you under weakening association and influence (1 Corinthians 15:33)?
8) Does it bring upon you an unequal yoke and place you at a disadvantage in serving the Lord (2 Corinthians 6:14-18)?[3]

None of these passages ever justifies sin. We must remember that God regulates morals—not us. Based on the principles God has revealed, we must weigh our actions and make our decisions based on what He said! That, more than anything, will help us know where to "draw the line."

---

[3] Adapted from *The New Testament Church* by R. Cogdill

Chapter Fifteen:
Overcoming the World

Each new day that we are given is full of opportunity as well as challenges. God has seen to that. How are we to possibly to overcome the world as it is so big and powerful? Trying to do so on our own is just asking for trouble. Thankfully, our God is faithful and provides the way so that we can overcome the negative forces arrayed against by our flesh, the world with its robust systems and last but not least, the Devil and the massive army that he has deployed against us. If it were naturally speaking, we should just throw the proverbial towel in and admit defeat. BUT, God has done amazing things when he prepared our gear for us and with what strength he can give us. There is only one possible way to overcome, and that is through the blood of our beloved Savior Jesus Christ.

Remember, in the last section talking about Jesus as our example? Well, he wiped the ground with Satan and defeated him decisively when he was put to death and rose again through the power of the Father. He not only beat the Devil every time that he faced him but in his death, he trounced the principalities and powers and took them captive to do His will! Can you even begin to see the fear in Satan's camp on that first day of the week after his crucifixion? Here they probably were just getting done with their victory celebrations when some poor little demon had the job to go tell Satan that the tomb was open and was empty! There it was, the absolute shock among Satan's forces. Jesus Christ, through his death and burial, was the payment for everyone's sin, and Satan's power was shattered—right in front of him! Well, that victory can be ours if we seek God when he may be found. All we have to do to receive that is to learn God's word and obey it to the best of our ability! Jesus said: John 15:14, *if you love me, you will keep my commands.* Now, granted, it is hard at first when we are ignorant and don't know what that entails. That is the first step in overcoming the world. We begin to overcome the influence of the world by taking the proper attitude toward it. Have you ever heard the phrase that "your altitude is dependent upon your attitude"? Well, it's entirely accurate. 1 John 2:15-17:

> *Love not the world, neither the things that are in the world. If any man love the world, the love of the Father is not in him. For all that is in the world, the lust of the flesh and the lust of the eyes and the vainglory of life is not of the Father but is of the world. And the world passeth away, and the lust thereof: but he that doeth the will of God abideth forever.*

It tells us a lot. Romans 12:1-2 tells us that

> *I beseech you therefore, brethren, by the mercies of God, to present your bodies a living sacrifice, holy, acceptable to God, which is your spiritual service. And be not fashioned according to this world: but be ye transformed by the renewing of your mind, that ye may prove what is the good and acceptable and perfect will of God.*

This change actually begins in Romans 8:5-10.

> *For they that are after the flesh mind the things of the flesh; but they that are after the Spirit the things of the Spirit. For the mind of the flesh is death; but the mind of the Spirit is life and peace: because the mind of the flesh is enmity against God; for it is not subject to the law of God, neither indeed can it be: and they that are in the flesh cannot please God. But ye are not in the flesh but in the Spirit if so be that the Spirit of God dwelleth in you. But if any man hath not the Spirit of Christ, he is none of his. And if Christ is in you, the body is dead because of sin; but the spirit is life because of righteousness.*

Are you starting to see it now? What was fuzzy and unclear is gradually coming into focus. God has let us in on the secret that he has been keeping for millennia. We know that the prophets as well as the angels have desired to know this information for thousands of years and could not. It was not the right time, the conditions were not favorable, and everyone had to wait. Patience!

Okay, drop the question...how are we to overcome the world? What must we do?

Luke 17:3 <u>Take heed to yourselves</u>: if thy brother sins, rebuke him; and if he repents, forgive him.

1 Timothy 4:16 <u>Take heed to thyself</u>, and thy teaching. Continue in these things; for in doing this thou shalt save both thyself and them that hear thee.

Acts 20:28 <u>Take heed unto yourselves</u>, and to all the flock, in which the Holy Spirit hath made you bishops, to feed the church of the Lord which he purchased with his own blood.

We are to watch ourselves, that is the first responsibility!
Next step after we get a leash on ourselves is: Romans 6:12-14

<u>Let not sin therefore reign in your mortal body</u>, that ye should obey the lusts thereof: neither present your members unto sin as instruments of unrighteousness; but present yourselves unto God, as alive from the dead, and your members as instruments of righteousness unto God. For sin shall not he dominion over you: for ye are not under the law but under grace.

We must attack and offset the power of the sin and worldliness that would overcome each of us. We must make a radical commitment when dealing with these matters. Some have fallen back and been consumed. Never turn your back to the enemy, never! In this battle with sin, always face towards it. Ask God for strength to deal with the situation, pray without ceasing, and move forward.

Our commitment must be complete; we must be committed to offsetting the world in our bodies. We can't control what happens outside of us, but we can on the inside. This is how we begin the fight. It starts from within ourselves. Again, I repeat a verse that we have seen before: Romans 12:1

I beseech you therefore, brethren, by the mercies of God, to present your bodies a <u>living sacrifice</u>, holy, acceptable to God, which is your spiritual service.

A living sacrifice—that entails self-control!

Galatians 5:24 And they that are of Christ Jesus have <u>crucified the flesh</u> with the passions and the lusts thereof.

Galatians 6:14 But far be it from me to glory, save in the cross of our Lord Jesus Christ, through which the world hath been crucified unto me, and I unto the world.

These surely are not popular, nor easy things to do, but if you want to fight back, this is the pathway to do so. Get control of the only thing you can—yourself—and start the fight there. Remember, God has called us to a life of holiness, and this is that path! (1 Peter 1:16 *because it is written,* Ye shall be holy; for I am holy.) Our very thought processes have to be changed; we must adopt His kind of thinking. Eph. 4:22-23

that ye put away, as concerning your former manner of life, the old man, that waxeth corrupt after the lusts of deceit; and that ye be renewed in the spirit of your mind.

We must understand that this change will come gradually and only through effort on our part. But by putting forth the effort and praying, it can and will be affected. 1 Thessalonians 5:17 reminds us to *pray without ceasing,* and so we should.

Now, we must begin to talk about the conscience and its work in guiding us. It is a God-given tool that will go far in guiding us, BUT there are some things that need to be noticed. Our conscience must be educated according to what God's word declares as proper. Jiminy Cricket told you to "let your conscience be your guide," and that is a wise piece of knowledge, but we must know, and apply God's word when doing the training. What the world finds as proper is a l-o-n-g shot from what God claims as to the truth! We must learn the Lord's will or end up being in opposition to what He says as is moral! There can be much danger that we must be aware of. As an example: Titus 1:15 tells us:

To the pure all things are pure: but to them that are defiled and unbelieving nothing is pure, but both their mind and their conscience are defiled.

That can happen, so we must be careful about how we train it. Is my conscience to be your guide in such matters?

Romans 14:13 Let us not, therefore, judge one another anymore: but judge ye this rather, that no man put a stumbling-block in his brother's way, or an occasion of falling.

That is a fantastic piece of divine wisdom—don't judge and put no stumbling block in another's way. All very safe and very doable.

Next, How am I to respond to someone whose conscience causes him to "draw the line" in a different place than I do? Well, the divine answer to that is Romans 15:1-7

> *Now we that are strong ought to bear the infirmities of the weak, and not to please ourselves. Let each one of us please his neighbor for that which is good, unto edifying. For Christ also pleased not himself; but, as it is written, The reproaches of them that reproached thee fell upon me. For whatsoever things were written aforetime were written for our learning, that through patience and through comfort of the scriptures we might have hope. Now the God of patience and of comfort grant you to be of the same mind one with another according to Christ Jesus: that with one accord ye may with one mouth glorify the God and Father of our Lord Jesus Christ. Wherefore receive ye one another, even as Christ also received you, to the glory of God.*

Such wisdom must come from God, the author of **all** wisdom.

The dangerous consequences of "judging other people's actions by my own conscience" is quite clear, and that is in the following examples: Joshua 22:1-34, 1 Corinthians 8:1-13, 1 Corinthians 10:23-33, Romans 14:1-23. Due to the length of each of these passages, I cannot lay them out, as attractive as that might be.

These passages never justify sin. We must remember that God regulates morals—not us. Based on the principles God has revealed, we must weigh our actions and make our decisions based on what He said! That, more than anything, will help us know where to "draw the line." Let us then resolve to follow that divinely given wisdom on to its ultimate revelation in the kingdom of our Lord Jesus Christ.

We then begin to overcome the influence of the world by having the proper attitude towards it in our own lives. Our responses to it should be very determined and we must have a very decided response. That is:

And I am no more in the world, and these are in the world, and I come to thee. Holy Father, keep them in thy name which thou hast given me, that they may be one, even as we are. While I was with them, I kept them in thy name which thou hast given me: and I guarded them, and not one of them perished, but the son of perdition; that the scripture might be fulfilled. But now I come to thee; and these things I speak in the world, that they may have my joy made full in themselves. I have given them thy word; and the world hated them, because they are not of the world, even as I am not of the world. I pray not that thou shouldest take them from the world, but that thou shouldest keep them from the evil one. They are not of the world even as I am not of the world. Sanctify them in the truth: thy word is truth. As thou didst send me into the world, even so sent I them into the world. And for their sakes I sanctify myself, that they themselves also may be sanctified in truth. Neither for these only do I pray, but for them also that believe on me through their word; that they may all be one; even as thou, Father, art in me, and I in thee, that they also may be in us: that the world may believe that thou didst send me. John 17:11-21.

This passage covers a lot of ground, but it talks about sending and being sent. It talks about us being guarded against the evil one as well as several other topics. I John 2:15-17 appears again, verifying how important those verses are in dealing with our enemies.

Love not the world, neither the things that are in the world. If any man love the world, the love of the Father is not in him. For all that is in the world, the lust of the flesh and the lust of the eyes and the vainglory of life is not of the Father but is of the world. And the world passeth away, and the lust thereof: but he that doeth the will of God abideth forever.

I don't ever mean to use scripture unnecessarily. This set is vital in our dealings with those who are still in the world.

Let us take heed to its warnings and wisely return to our Lord for safety and sustenance. Also, protection from those enemies. This leads us to ask, "How can we overtake those enemies? "

100

Luke 17:3 Take heed to yourselves: if thy brother sin, rebuke him; and if he repent, forgive him.

There again—take heed to thyself. We attack and offset the power of sin and worldliness that would overcome each of us:

Romans 6:12-14. Let not sin therefore reign in your mortal body, that ye should obey the lusts thereof: neither present your members unto sin as instruments of unrighteousness; but present yourselves unto God, as alive from the dead, and your members as instruments of righteousness unto God. For <u>sin shall not have dominion over you</u>: for ye are not under the law but under grace.

We start to overcome when we gain control of ourselves. Sin is next to fall. By watching and praying as well as practicing mastering ourselves, our commitment to this is not namby-pamby but strong, to the overcoming of strongholds. 2 Corinthians 10:4.

We are called upon to make this radical commitment, and so we do. I believe that total and complete effort should be expended on our part, and we should strive to see if there are more things that can be done than just what scripture tells us to do.

Galatians 5:24 And they that are of Christ Jesus have crucified the flesh with the passions and the lusts thereof.

6:14 also says:

But far be it from me to glory, save in the cross of our Lord Jesus Christ, through which the world hath been crucified unto me, and I unto the world.

Once we have managed to get our thoughts in line and then seek to bring our behavior with it, we can then strike out to accomplish the modification of our lives. Now, keep in mind, you are not going to achieve this without some other difficulties. Satan will seek to drag you back to the experience that you were living along before you tried to obey the Lord in your life. This will happen as sure as the sun rises in the morning. So, you will then be fighting against both your tendencies but also the Devil in your life. On your own, this would be an impossibility, but our Lord makes all things possible! His strength will be your strength, and you can and will overcome through the blood of the Lamb!

Another question that comes to mind that needs to be addressed is: How do we maintain that change in our thinking and actions? This answer is vital to our spiritual health, and it is Colossians 3:1-4

> *If then ye were raised together with Christ, seek the things that are above, where Christ is, seated on the right hand of God. Set your mind on the things that are above, not on the things that are upon the earth. For ye died, and your life is hid with Christ in God.*

Philippians 3:13-14 says

> *Brethren, I count not myself yet to have laid hold: but one thing I do, forgetting the things which are behind, and stretching forward to the things which are before. I press on toward the goal unto the prize of the high calling of God in Christ Jesus.*

These two sets of verses give us a healthy look at the subject, so let us take heed to their directions and strive to *work out your own salvation with fear and trembling.* (Philippians 2:12.)

Now, to maintain the change in our thinking long-term, let us seek Hebrews 10:35-39:

> *Cast not away, therefore, your boldness, which hath great recompense of reward. For ye have need of patience, that, having done the will of God, ye may receive the promise. For yet a very little while, He that cometh shall come, and shall not tarry. But my righteous one shall live by faith: And if he shrink back, my soul hath no pleasure in him. But we are not of them that shrink back unto perdition; but of them that have faith unto the saving of the soul.*

It can and must be maintained long term. God commands this, and so we must do it.

To conclude this matter, let us turn back to the word of God and don't let the world around you squeeze you into its mold. The temptations of the world that would draw us away from God are not stronger than God's pull on us. Since we are the ones who choose either God or the world, their power is sufficient to entice us away from God. We can overcome or be overcome by this world—it is up to us.

Chapter Sixteen:
Resist the Devil and He Will Flee

I know that I have mentioned it several times, but I hope that I have not given anyone the impression of either extreme of thinking the devil is just some force, or if he is a being, he's that comical guy with the pitchfork and horns and the other extreme that he is co-equal with God, a dark side to God's light and is all powerful like God. Both are wrong, wrong, WRONG. He is a being that although he is more powerful than we are, is vastly inferior to Him who conquered him, that is Jesus Christ. With that said, let us take a good in depth look at how he can be resisted and even to made to flee! (James 4:7)

The right question is, who has the greater pull over us-Satan or God? John 10:27-29

> *My sheep hear my voice, and I know them, and they follow me: and I give unto them eternal life; and they shall never perish, and no one shall snatch them out of my hand. My Father, who hath given them unto me, is greater than all; and no one is able to snatch them out of the Father's hand.*

That settles that pretty conclusively. Next, knowing that Jesus has more power, how did that happen?

> ***Matthew 12:29*** *Or how can one enter into the house of the strong man, and spoil his goods, except he first <u>bind the strong man</u>? and then he will spoil his house?*

> ***John 12:31*** *Now is the judgment of this world: now shall the <u>prince of this world be cast out</u>.*

> ***Colossians 2:15*** <u>*having despoiled the principalities and the powers,*</u> *he made a show of them openly, triumphing over them in it.*

> ***1 John 3:8*** *he that doeth sin is of the devil; for the devil sinneth from the beginning. To this end was the Son of God manifested, that he might <u>destroy the works of the devil</u>.*

Hebrews 2:14 *Since then the children are sharers in flesh and blood, he also himself in like manner partook of the same; that through death he might <u>bring to naught</u> him that had the power of death, that is, the devil*

Lastly, in this section, Jesus has overcome and has empowered His church to overcome. In Matthew 16:18 we read:

And I also say unto thee, that thou art Peter, and upon this rock I will build my church; and the <u>gates of Hades shall not prevail against it.</u>

As discussed earlier, we know that of ourselves we have less power than Satan and his minions, but through God's great kindness and grace, we are given power through Jesus victory over Satan so that we can resist him. That does not mean we can try foolishness like was shown in the book of Acts by exorcists:

Acts 19:13-16 But certain also of the strolling Jews, exorcists, took upon them to name over them that had the evil spirits the name of the Lord Jesus, saying, I adjure you by Jesus whom Paul preacheth. And there were seven sons of one Sceva, a Jew, a chief priest, who did this. And the evil spirit answered and said unto them, Jesus I know, and Paul I know; but who are ye? And the man in whom the evil spirit was leaped on them, and mastered both of them, and prevailed against them so that they fled out of that house naked and wounded.

Now stunts like that are going to do nothing but cause problems. The relationship with Jesus was true, but these characters did not have it, and they paid quite dearly for their supposed "power" over evil spirits."

We are given instructions on how to resist, and these are they:

James 4:7-9 Be subject therefore unto God but resist the devil, and he will flee from you. Draw nigh to God, and he will draw nigh to you. Cleanse your hands, ye sinners; and purify your hearts, ye doubleminded. Be afflicted, and mourn, and weep: let your laughter be turned to mourning and your joy to heaviness. Humble yourselves in the sight of the Lord, and he shall exalt you.

Yes, you see where it tells us to resist, but there are a bunch of other instructions which are right there alongside it. We are to draw nigh to God, cleanse ourselves—see 1 Peter 1:19: we are to mourn for our sinful behavior. And most important of all we are to humble ourselves to be everything that Satan cannot be. These commands all come together and should be worked on in our lives. It takes a lot of hard work to gain these ideals. Don't become discouraged, but daily—day by day—we are to fight this battle. Only through obedience to all of these things can we hope to overcome our adversary. Leave any out, and you are asking for trouble!

Turning to Ephesians 4:27, we can see that: *neither give place to the devil*. This advice tells us not to give in to him because he will do nothing but strive to harm us in any way that he can. In Romans, we are told that we are more than conquerors through Jesus Christ. Jesus won that victory at a steep price, so don't make little His victory by giving in to Satan.

We need to be active in the battle between good and evil. Being passive only brings set-backs. In Ephesians 6:11-12 God tells us:

> *Put on the whole armor of God, that ye may be able to stand against the wiles of the devil. For our wrestling is not against flesh and blood, but against the principalities, against the powers, against the world-rulers of this darkness, against the spiritual hosts of wickedness in the heavenly places.*

Does this sound like you can sit back and watch? No, absolutely not. We are at war. You can't hide from the conflict. Now it is time to prepare and get involved!

Principalities are rulers, princes, or preeminent ones. The word appears to be used of spiritual beings, most likely angels. Jude spoke of the angels which kept not their first estate but left their own habitation in Jude 6.

These same beings are identified often in the writings of Paul as powerful personages.

> *To the intent that now unto the principalities and powers in heavenly places might be known by the church the manifold wisdom of God (Ephesians 3:10).*

> *For by him were all things created, that are in heaven, and that are in earth, visible and invisible, whether they be*

thrones, or dominions, or principalities, or powers: all things were created by him, and for him (Colossians 1:16).

Blotting out the handwriting of ordinances that was against us, which was contrary to us, and took it out of the way, nailing it to his cross; and having spoiled principalities and powers, he made a show of them openly, triumphing over them in it (Colossians 2:14-15).

For I am persuaded, that neither death, nor life, nor angels, nor principalities, nor powers, nor things present, nor things to come, nor height, nor depth, nor any other creature, shall be able to separate us from the love of God, which is in Christ Jesus our Lord (Rom. 8:38-39).

Powers are authorities or potentates. These have had the right to act as a result of their freedom to direct others. In those same passages cited, they also appear to be spiritual beings, perhaps both good and bad angels. **World rulers of this darkness** are tyrants. They no doubt include Satan himself who is, at least in some senses, the ruler of this world John 12:31; 14:30; 16:11; 2 Corinthians 4:4. It appears from the context, which says that *we wrestle not against flesh and blood,* that Paul is not talking about human kings and presidents. He is discussing spiritual rulers who act for Satan to bring the world under his control. That pits them against Christians and identifies them as forces to be conquered in the great battle for the soul.[4]

Now, I am **so glad** that I can finally describe how we can go on the offensive against Satan and his hordes. God hath given us the offensive weapons to do some severe damage when facing Satan and his "children." We will spend some time explaining each piece of kit and how it either protects us or gives us offensive capabilities. We learn a valuable lesson in **2 Corinthians 10:3-4**

For though we walk in the flesh, we do not war according to the flesh (for the weapons of our warfare are not of the flesh, but mighty before God to the casting down of strongholds),

These two verses affirm that we are at war and must participate. Let's see what the Scripture tells us next. We read

---

[4] *Ephesians*, Caldwell (Truth Publications), p. 309.

Ephesians 6:13-18 Wherefore take up the whole armor of God, that ye may be able to withstand in the evil day, and, having done all, to stand. Stand therefore, having girded your loins with truth, and having put on the breastplate of right-eousness, and having shod your feet with the preparation of the gospel of peace; withal taking up the shield of faith, wherewith ye shall be able to quench all the fiery darts of the evil one. And take the helmet of salvation, and the sword of the Spirit, which is the word of God: with all prayer and sup-plication praying at all seasons in the Spirit, and watching thereunto in all perseverance and supplication for all the saints,

We can see from verse 13 that we are commanded to take up God's armor and that:

1) There is to be an evil day.

2) We are commanded to stand. These commands directly imply that we are to take up the provided armor and get into the thick of the fight!

Perhaps before I begin giving descriptions of armor, we can say a little about it, and the ancient soldier who was tasked with wear-ing that armor and using the weapons

The Apostle Paul was a world traveler in the first century. His travels took him from Tarshish in the Taurus mountains to the shores of the Roman homeland. If there was one thing that Paul knew it was what a Roman soldier and his gear looked like. They could be found from the Holy Land up to the shores of Britain. Their uniforms were alike enough to give one general impression, and Paul gives it in Ephesians six when he was teaching us about our gear and its use.

The first item to receive his attention is the belt of the truth. ***The belt of truth***. As the soldier's belt was for support and protection of the lower abdomen, so the belt of truth aids and protects the child of God. *Ye shall know the truth, and the truth shall make you free* (Jn. 8:32). The belt was the basis of everything else that a soldier would wear. His breastplate, especially; was attached to that belt, and without it, all would simply fall to the ground. If a belt were lost, the soldier would be lost because he had nothing by which to anchor everything else. The truth is the same for us. The fact of our lives is the basis for nearly everything. Without it, we could not participate on God's side in the battle. We have read that Satan is the father of lies so that will undo any Christian who tells lies.

The second most important piece of kit is the **breastplate of righteousness** how to be righteous before God is found in the word of God, the gospel.

> *For therein is revealed a righteousness of God from faith to faith: as it is written, But the righteous shall live by faith (Romans 1:17)*

To have righteousness, is to have the supreme desire to be right and to do right. It is a conscious decision to put on the new man, that after God hath been created in righteousness and holiness of truth (Ephesians. 4:24). We must always want righteousness and to strive to be righteous before God. This, like the breastplate, covers our vital areas and gives us the strength to carry on.

Third **The shoes of the gospel of peace**. Shoes protect the feet, aid in standing firm, and carrying the battle to the enemy. The gospel of peace (with God) is the force we must use to overcome the disruptive influences of Satan. It is God's power to save, but only to those who believe and live by it (Romans 1:16-17).

> *Establish my footsteps in thy word; And let not any iniquity have dominion over me. Psalm. 119:133*

Fourth **The shield of faith.** The Roman shield was four feet high and protected from flaming arrows and other dangers. *Faith comes by hearing and hearing by the word of God* (Romans 10:17). If the Christian leaves his faith on the ground, rather than taking it up, Satan is sure to gain the advantage.

> *Thou art my hiding-place and my shield: I hope in thy word (Psalm. 119:114).*

The Roman shield had many uses. It could be put toward the front to extinguish flaming arrows and darts. It could also be lifted up above the troops effectively placing a roof of safety from plunging fire. The shields were of universal shape and size.

In our spiritual warfare, we use the shield of faith to extinguish the flaming darts that are hurled by our enemies. How many times have we used our faith to extinguish some terrible blow which the enemy would send against us? Faith shields its owner from all types of trials and temptations.

Fifth ***The helmet of salvation***

> *1 Thess. 5:8. But let us, since we are of the day, be sober, putting on the breastplate of faith and love; and for a helmet, the hope of salvation.*

The helmet guards the head, a vital organ. How many soldiers have died on the battlefield simply because they didn't have their helmets on? The word of God guarding the mind will keep Satan from dealing a death blow.

Sixth ***The sword of the Spirit***, which is the word of God. The sword is offensive and defensive. Jesus forcefully resisted Satan with the truth (Matthew. 4:1-11), and we can do the same. If you don't take up the word of God, how can you possibly have success against the Adversary?

> *Thy word have I laid up in my heart, that I might not sin against thee (Psalm. 119:11).*

The word of God answers all questions and puts disputes to an end. In the spiritual realm, they want nothing to do with hearing God's word because it is the last straw, the full end of all wrangling and disputing. When it is used, all conflict comes to a halt — one in victory and joy, the other in defeat and anguish.

How does one equip himself with the whole armor of God? Bible study is the starting place. What you know about God and His will is found in the Bible. The Bible tells you all you need to know about the Enemy and how to defeat him.

> "But study alone won't get the job done. Memorizing Scripture is a good habit, but the word must be put into practice, not just in mind. The word only helps those *who by reason of use have their senses exercised to discern good and evil* (Hebrews 5:14). David couldn't use Saul's armor because he had not "tested it" (I Samuel 17:39). Too many Christians cannot withstand in the evil day in the heat of battle because they haven't sufficiently tested the armor of God. Would not it be great if all you had to do to beat Satan was to hold up a Bible or quote a passage? You can quote James

4:7 all day long, but if you do not do some resisting, the devil will devour you!

It is impossible to overemphasize the importance of prayer, deep-seated, sincere, genuinely, spiritual praying. Proper prayer is essential to gaining the advantage over Satan."[5]

Satan is the most potent foe we will ever have to face, but through Christ, we have the strength to resist him. We can be victorious over Satan—but not with some half-hearted effort! Satan is a coward who can be put to flight by strong conviction and resistance to him and his temptations. Have you put him to flight yet?

---

[5] Robert Gabhart Page 177 of 1998 Florida College. Lectures

Chapter Seventeen:
Take Heed Lest Ye Fall

Well, the preparation is over, the combat fought and won. What is next? What else do I need to be doing? There always has to be something needing attention in spiritual matters.

There is, and it is a big something. When it comes to dealing with our chief adversary, Satan, there is always something new that needs attention. You may have defeated him in one matter or another. He isn't dead or gone. You must take heed lest you fall. There is so much danger right now—in the flush of victory that one would have a hard time taking it all in.

1 Corinthians 10:12-13 Wherefore let him that thinketh he standeth take heed lest he falls. There hath no temptation taken you but such as man can bear: but God is faithful, who will not suffer you to be tempted above that ye are able; but will with the temptation also make the way of escape, that ye may be able to endure it.

Just when you think that you have gotten past the temptations, it starts all over again. He will be after you, trying to avenge the defeat that you handed him a bit ago. It rarely stops so be ready for the next one. God is prepared to help you get past the next one. He is always faithful to help and guide you when the next temptation comes.

We read in the Bible that God was with the children of Israel, and yet they ended up dying in the wilderness. What was that situation all about? Well, scripture tells us that they lusted after evil things and turned their backs on God. Who do you think was leading them into sin? It sure wasn't God. He was busy trying to help and provide for their needs as well as to keep them on the right path going forward. Someone had to be behind the transgression and can you think of who that might be? One guess. Yes, Satan was behind the scenes pushing them towards their transgression. We read a little about this in our New Testament.

Romans 11:20 Well; by their unbelief, they were broken off, and thou standest by thy faith. Be not highminded, but fear:

Why should we fear? What is this about, and how does it have anything to do with us? It does because God put off his people that sinned without repentance. This is the natural olive branch that was cut off. We are the wild olive branch that he grafted in. This can be found in Romans chapter eleven. In verses 21-24, we see:

> *for if God spared not the natural branches, neither will he spare thee. Behold then the goodness and severity of God: toward them that fell, severity; but toward thee, God's goodness, <u>if thou continue</u> in his goodness: otherwise thou also shalt be cut off. And they also, if they continue not in their unbelief, shall be grafted in: for God is able to graft them in again. For if thou wast cut out of that which is by nature a wild olive tree, and wast grafted contrary to nature into a good olive tree; how much more shall these, which are the natural branches, be grafted into their own olive tree?*

Satan's main task is to get you to sin to the point where God casts you off and removes your olive branch from the tree. That is pretty plain and simple to see. To get a better idea, read the entire chapter to get the context right. Anyway, his goal is to destroy you. He does not have the power to directly, so he tries to get God to cast you off. THAT is why we need to take heed.

Another example is given in 1 Corinthians, chapter nine. It also needs us to take heed to the warnings that are being given to us by God. It has been said that God needs only to tell us once, and it is our responsibility to take it from there. Well, God warns us all over the place in the New Testament about paying attention or taking heed. Even the Apostle Paul says so in 1 Corinthians 9 in various locations in various ways. Should we ignore that—or any warning? There has to be an excellent reason for this.

It most surely is possible to fall from grace after being saved by God. In Hebrews 6:4-6 we read:

> *For as touching those who were once enlightened and tasted of the heavenly gift, and were made partakers of the Holy Spirit, and tasted the good word of God, and the powers of the age to come, <u>and then fell away</u>, it is impossible to renew them*

again unto repentance; seeing they crucify to themselves the Son of God afresh, and put him to an open shame.

To our Calvinistic friends, this is unanswerable.

2 Peter 2:20-22 says:

For if, after they have escaped the defilements of the world through the knowledge of the Lord and Savior Jesus Christ, they are again entangled therein and overcome, the last state is become worse with them than the first. For it were better for them not to have known the way of righteousness, than, after knowing it, to turn back from the holy commandment delivered unto them. It has happened unto them according to the true proverb, The dog turning to his own vomit again, and the sow that had washed to wallowing in the mire.

Galatians 5:4 adds:

Ye are severed from Christ, ye who would be justified by the law; ye are fallen away from grace.

What kind of answer can you have to these verses? You must understand the word of God and comply with its commandments. Jesus said in John 14:15: *If ye love me, ye will keep my commandments.* And also in 15:14: *Ye are my friends, if ye do the things which I command you.* If he is the only path to salvation, we most definitely need to listen to his commands.

Now that we have, in our minds, overcome sin and are walking in the light; well, surprise, surprise surprise: that is where the danger is the greatest. This is your softest point. You don't realize how weak and undefended you are. Your guard is down; you are not looking through the word of God like you would be if you were in "battle" mode. Paul talked about it 2 Timothy 4 where he used so many different ways to exhibit his thoughts—the farmer, the soldier, the athlete. These were brilliant methods of adorning the word. Why go through so much trouble to present the ideas that he was trying to display if it were not possible to fall short? There are dangers inherent with this war that we have been dragged into. Romans 2:17-24 gives some idea regarding our spiritual lives. That says:

> *But if thou bearest the name of a Jew, and restest upon the law, and gloriest in God, and knowest his will, and approvest the things that are excellent, being instructed out of the law, and art confident that thou thyself art a guide of the blind, a light of them that are in darkness, a corrector of the foolish, a teacher of babes, having in the law the form of knowledge and of the truth; thou, therefore, that teachest another, teachest thou, not thyself? Thou that preachest a man should not steal, dost thou steal? thou that sayest a man should not commit adultery, dost thou commit adultery? thou that abhorrest idols, dost thou rob temples? thou who gloriest in the law, through thy transgression of the law dishonorest thou God?*

That is dangerous enough to have your branch removed or perhaps your candlestick?

> *Revelation 2:5 Remember therefore whence thou art fallen, and repent and do the first works; or else I come to thee, and will move thy candlestick out of its place, except thou repent.*

A question recently came up in a class that would be good to ask and answer here: "Does God show any special favor to His children, just because they are His children? "

Romans 2:11-14 were the best answer that I can find to it.

> *For there is no respect of persons with God. For as many as have sinned without law shall also perish without the law: and as many as have sinned under the law shall be judged by the law; for not the hearers of the law are just before God, but the doers of the law shall be justified:*

Apparently not, at least as far as I could find. Then again, there are a good number of verses telling us of his love and care, so I will say yes, he does. He loves us all and sends rain and sunshine to each and everyone or us. That is both reassuring and upsetting as we consider its implications. God is faithful and will meet your needs no matter who you are. That is good news!

Returning from our little distraction, there are several answers given about our taking heed lest we fall. What are some things that we should be watching for? Well, the first can be found in Luke 22:31:

Simon, Simon, behold, Satan asked to have you, that he might sift you as wheat: but I made supplication for thee, that thy faith fail not; and do thou, when once thou hast turned again, establish thy brethren.

Satan is still involved. He had to ask permission to "sift" the apostles like wheat and received an answer "No!!" from our Lord.

Acts 20:29 I know that after my departing grievous wolves shall enter in among you, not sparing the flock

Paul is warning about false teachers like we have to look for even at this late hour.

Matthew 13:21 yet hath he not root in himself, but endureth for a while; and when tribulation or persecution ariseth because of the word, straightway he stumbleth.

Trials and temptations of this life can lead us away.

2 Timothy 4:19 for Demas forsook me, having loved this present world, and went to Thessalonica; Crescens to Galatia, Titus to Dalmatia.

Love for this present life can also cause us to walk away.

1 John 2:15-17 Love not the world, neither the things that are in the world. If any man love the world, the love of the Father is not in him. For all that is in the world, the lust of the flesh and the lust of the eyes and the vainglory of life is not of the Father but is of the world. And the world passeth away, and the lust thereof: but he that doeth the will of God abideth for ever.

Love of the world, the Flesh and the Devil can turn us around till we can only see those things.

Romans 8:15 For ye received not the spirit of bondage again unto fear; but ye received the spirit of adoption, whereby we cry, Abba, Father.

We return to whatever bondage we were in previous to our conversion.

These five items are by no means comprehensive but will give a good idea of some of the traps that are laid outside of Christ. It is an outstanding list that we ought to really look at and then go to the final section of this rather large study. This is something that we ought to do on a relatively often basis. That is to give ourself, thoughts and motives a regular comprehensive examination. In this world, the medical community urges the population to see their physician for a comprehensive exam. In 2 Cor. 13:5-6. We read:

> *Try your own selves, whether ye are in the faith; prove your own selves. Or know ye not as to your own selves, that Jesus Christ is in you? unless indeed ye be reprobate. But I hope that ye shall know that we are not reprobate.*

We need to examine ourselves because we are flawed beings who cannot guide themselves. Jeremiah 10:23 tells us why:

> *O Jehovah, I know that the way of man is not in himself: it is not in man that walketh to direct his steps.*

That is why we simply cannot keep on the path by ourselves. God must lead us if we are to have any hope of making it to heaven. The standard is found in James 1:22-25.

> *But be ye doers of the word, and not hearers only, deluding your own selves. For if any one is a hearer of the word and not a doer, he is like unto a man beholding his natural face in a mirror: for he beholdeth himself, and goeth away, and straightway forgetteth what manner of man he was.*

We must be doers of the word and not lazy as is our tendency. There is much to do; there's work on every hand. Hark the cry for workers rings throughout the land. Then let us get to do what is right and follow our blessed Lord's commands.

We know ourselves, and our real condition before God is the first step in doing what is right. When we examine ourselves, we may find ourselves to be satisfactory, or we may find ourselves to be condemned—but by all means, we need to find out now, before the Lord exposes us·at the end. 1 Corinthians 4:5 tells us:

> *Wherefore judge nothing before the time, until the Lord come, who will both bring to light the hidden things of darkness and make manifest the counsels of the hearts; and then shall each man have his praise from God.*

Complacency and overconfidence can cause us to fall just as surely as sin or false teaching. We must guard against becoming our own worst enemy!

This short study is designed to help us to know what is the real situation in our world today. I hope that in searching the scriptures, we might find life and the power to fight and overcome the enemy of souls. We thank our beloved creator, who has given us all things to enjoy.

A Short
Encyclopedia of
Occult Practices

Chapter Eighteen:
The Rising Force that is the Occult

The world in which we live is increasingly hostile to us and openly embracing the world of the occult as revealed in the lives of those around us. The entertainment media is full of news from such motion pictures as the *Harry Potter* series or *The Exorcist* book. Witchcraft and sorcery are "in," and those of us who oppose such acts are guilty of "hate crimes." Things which God openly condemned in the Old Testament are embraced by today's culture. It appears that the fine veneer of civility from earlier days is increasingly off of society as it rushes headlong to destruction. This was revealed in the scriptures for those who have such practices.

The Bible speaks of two kingdoms in Colossians 1:13-14

> *"He has delivered us from the domain (power ASV) of darkness and transferred us to the kingdom of his beloved Son, in whom we have redemption, the forgiveness of sins."*

Notice the difference between the domain of darkness and the kingdom of his dear Son. There are only two choices-1) domain (or kingdom) of darkness 2) kingdom of God's beloved Son.

Without going into depth on how one enters, or rather, is added (Acts 2:41) to the kingdom by the Lord, we do know that when one enters the kingdom of God, he or she departs from the kingdom of darkness. This departure is against the will of the leader of that kingdom, Satan. It is Satan's will to recapture this "escapee" and to stop any further "captures" by his enemy, God. With this in mind, let us look at the warfare which continues between the forces of God and the forces of Satan.

Those who have any familiarity with scripture are aware that we are told in Ephesians 6:10-18:

> *Finally, be strong in the Lord and in the strength of his might. Put on the whole armor of God, that you may be able to stand against the schemes of the devil. For we do not wrestle against flesh and blood, but against the rulers, against the authorities, against the cosmic powers over this present dark-*

120

ness, against the spiritual forces of evil in the heavenly places. Therefore, take up the whole armor of God, that you may be able to withstand in the evil day, and having done all, to stand firm. Stand therefore, having fastened on the belt of truth, and having put on the breastplate of righteousness, and, as shoes for your feet, having put on the readiness given by the gospel of peace. In all circumstances take up the shield of faith, with which you can extinguish all the flaming darts of the evil one; and take the helmet of salvation, and the sword of the Spirit, which is the word of God, praying at all times in the Spirit, with all prayer and supplication. To that end keep alert with all perseverance, making supplication for all the saints.

Paul, the apostle, likens the Christian soldier to that with which he was very familiar, the Roman soldier. The Roman soldier was a common sight throughout the empire of that day, and all were familiar with them. Using the figure of this earthly soldier, Paul was able to convey to his readers the complete coverage the (heavenly) soldier of God receives if he were to use the armor in such a way as the Lord has directed.

A couple of things to note are that there is no coverage for the back, so the soldier always needed to face his adversary and not turn his back to the foe. Also, all the armor is defensive with one exception—the sword. The Roman soldiers carried a short stabbing-type of the sword in which it was necessary to be close to the foe. There were no" long-distance attacks" such as is common in our day. Back in those days, the soldier faced his foe face-to-face and fought in hand-to-hand combat. We need to be close to those we oppose and to use God's word (such as Jesus did) when facing our foe. Jesus dealt with Satan's onslaught as recorded, in Matthew chapter four by saying, "it is written." This is how we are to deal with our opponents. We are to use God's word in the same way that our Lord used it when Satan tempted him. As always, Jesus gave the perfect example of how we are to face the myriad of trials which we might face in our day to day lives. If we make a study of how Jesus lived and how he faced his trials, then we have a perfect pattern to follow when we face ours. As difficult as it is, it is vital that we keep our eyes upon him. He is our **good shepherd** (John 10:11;14), our **yoke bearer** (Matt. 11:29), our **light** (John 8:12), our **Savior** (Phil. 3:20). And, if we look unto him and *"casting all your anxieties on him because he cares for you"* (1 Peter 5:7), we will be able to face any threat or attack which will come our way. This is how we face the Kingdom of Darkness as we confront it throughout our lives. Our simple manner of life will bring us into conflict with the forces of the evil one. We then can overcome them by the blood of the lamb and the word of his testimony (Rev. 12:11).

We need to be continuously reminded that we are at war, and in this war, there are no "sidelines" or "noncombatants." We **all** are involved, and we need to keep our eyes and ears open and our prayer life a busy one as our strength is from above, and **by faith,** we can walk after the Spirit and not after the flesh. We **can** be well-pleasing to our heavenly father, and a scourge to his (and our enemies) provided we do things in his way and not our own. To God be the glory!!

It is our responsibility to be watchmen that are wide-awake and not "asleep at the wheel." Let us go forth, preaching the word in any way that we can and let us never forget that the enemy of our God is our enemy too.

We so often hear that "times are hard" and in hard times people do things that they would not normally do. Today there is a great curiosity to know things that really ought not to be known. We had known of times formerly when people sought this knowledge like the Gnostics of the early second and third century. And so on throughout the ages, there were movements, and people who wanted to know things that man ought not to know and that hunger seem to have been growing to the point where people are fascinated with the secret or more commonly called the Occult. Today, there is an intense hunger for the things which God has told mankind that is forbidden. In Deuteronomy 18:9-12, we read:

> *When thou art come into the land which Jehovah thy God giveth thee, thou shalt not learn to do after the abominations of those nations. There shall not be found with thee any one that maketh his son or his daughter to pass through the fire, one that useth divination, one that practiseth augury, or an enchanter, or a sorcerer, or a charmer, or a consulter with a familiar spirit, or a wizard, or a necromancer. For whosoever*

122

doeth these things is an abomination unto Jehovah: and because of these abominations, Jehovah thy God doth drive them out from before thee.

Here God was speaking to Israel, but the principles are the same across the board when dealing with the gospel dispensation. When God commands something, it isn't a suggestion or a "you ought to." but a command.

In our present age, a terrible spiritual vacuum exists in our land. Religion has declined as much as the occult has grown because people aren't satisfied with spiritual things as they exist and they want to find out in other ways—the ways which God has forbidden. They also are interested in physical pleasure and finding satisfaction in any way that they can. Also, they are dissatisfied with science and technology because they haven't brought the utopia that they have promised. We were raised to believe that the future held the answers, but whoever has those great answers isn't forthcoming at the speed which **we** desire. Lost in a spiritual void, our hearts long for some kind of reality apart from accountability to God and his word. Those are conditions that are nearly perfect for the growth of the occult and has fueled its growth tremendously. People are acting in pure contrariness to plain and simple logic. They do the most horrible things for the **least** practical reason. They have no idea, at least, to the authorities who arrest them for child murder, etc. etc. It is horrible and reprehensible, to say the least.

Today, undeniable evidence of the cult explosion pervades every aspect of our society, or rather, WORLD society. Occultism is similar to a giant spider-web going from city to city, nation to nation. Some have resisted better some, not so much. Back in Bible times in Revelation, Jesus told all the churches that some towns were some Satanic hosts.

Revelation 2:9: I know thy tribulation, and thy poverty (but thou art rich), and the blasphemy of them that say they are Jews, and they are not, but are a <u>synagogue of Satan</u>.

Revelation 2:13: I know where thou dwellest, even where <u>Satan's throne is</u>, and thou holdest fast my name and does not deny my faith, even in the days of Antipas my witness, my *faithful one, who was killed among you, <u>where Satan dwelleth.</u> Here are two, but I know that there are more of those type of descriptions.*

Why has this happened? Many, including myself, have attempted to give an apparent reason behind it. An obvious answer is that Satan and his cronies are behind it. Well, **they are behind it**. They have found a way to speak to the bait (remember my allusion to fishing) with some tasty treats that will make the "fish" take the bait, and when they do, it is over—**nearly**—because when they find out that they've been duped, it is too late to repent and be forgiven. Very slick but effective indeed. The reason I said "nearly" is because **I** am an unusual "fish." I got off the hook, and I have dedicated myself to teaching others about what these horrible creatures are that are prosecuting this war against my brothers and sisters of the human race. So, in the words of a television show and let's "get it," let's get going at spoiling the day for "the god of this world."

Chapter Nineteen:
A Doctrine of Demons

Those who are of the household of God are well acquainted—or rather *should be* well acquainted with the fact that there are "doctrines of demons" as referred to by the word of God. Scripture uses these exact words in **1 Timothy 4:1**

> *But the Spirit saith expressly, that in later times some shall fall away from the faith, giving heed to seducing spirits and doctrines of demons.*

The Lord went through the trouble of warning us of the fact that there will be things taught under the heading of "scripture" that are in fact nothing but the language of Satan—they are lies. Jesus told us that when Satan speaks, he lies because he is the father of lies. He is also a murderer—not that he has physically killed anyone—that *we* know of, but, by his lies to Eve, he caused their deaths, as well as introducing death to every one of their descendants, in that they all have sinned.

> *Romans 3:23: for all have sinned and fall short of the glory of God;*

> *Romans 6:23 tells us: For the wages of sin is death; but the free gift of God is eternal life in Christ Jesus our Lord.*

Let me correct the last sentence prior to the Bible references, because it, left to itself, is an "untruth." There is *one* of the descendants of Adam & Eve who was not killed by a lie, and mercifully, that one was Jesus Christ; son of man and Son of God. (Let me return to my subject at hand. I just get so delighted by the thought of the blessed Savior of a man—and deadly opponent of the "Doctrine of Demons.") In **1 Timothy 4:1-3**, we read:

> *Now the Spirit expressly says that in later times some will depart from the faith by devoting themselves to deceitful spirits and teachings (doctrine-ASV) of demons, through the insincerity of liars whose consciences are seared, who forbid marriage and require abstinence from foods that God created to*

be received with thanksgiving by those who believe and know the truth.

There are teachings which come from the evil one. These are often foisted off among the saints because the evil one tries to look like the saints. This can be seen in **2 Corinthians 11:13**:

For such men are false apostles, deceitful workmen, disguising themselves as apostles of Christ. And no wonder, for even Satan disguises himself as an angel of light. So, it is no surprise if his servants, also disguise themselves as servants of righteousness. Their end will correspond to their deeds.

Having shown this, let us take a look at a couple of these insidious teachings.

The early church had to deal with the heresy of Gnosticism. Gnosticism was a perversion of the truth as taught by certain men who felt that they had "special" or "secret" knowledge that lifted them above the ranks of "ordinary" Christians. This poison has continued throughout history in different times and different places. Although this teaching was opposed by the apostles directly in the first century, it has resulted in various false messiahs. An example of such in recent memory was Jim Jones in Guyana. David Koresh in Waco, Texas also had that "special knowledge" that only he felt he could dispense to willing and eager followers. Both, by the way, ended in death. Several hundred followers also were led into eternity in error. How much more demonic could one get?

Another form that developed was the doctrine that Jesus was "*a*" way, not the *only way* for man to be saved. This, of course, is in total opposition to what was taught by the Lord, where he said:

*I am the way, and the truth, and the life. No one comes to the Father except through me (**John 14:6**).*

Another doctrine which is from the very pits of Hell and is a variant of the above teaching says that another way to God can be found in such documents as the Koran, Hindu "scriptures" and what could be seen as any other writing which is, like above, "another way" to God. Apparently, according to these folks, we are all just one big happy family, all on the way to the same destination, only by a different route. We probably all have seen the giant billboard which declares: "Worship at The Church of Your Choice!" That is another example of this particular distasteful teaching. Besides the different religions being a different way, a closer variant is that the various denominations are all "branches of the same tree." The "Jehovah's Witnesses" are just a slightly different way to the truth as the Lord's church! Imagine that!! Is that distasteful to you as well? Now, we are bigoted if we have a problem with that! That is a doctrine of demons gone to seed. The land is full of such teachings. Now, can you imagine what would happen in the religious world if folks today saw things like they did in the time of the early Restoration Movement? The growth would be similar to as it was back in those days.

Again: "WORSHIP AT THE CHURCH OF YOUR CHOICE!!" How many multitudes believe that one church is as good as another? We face this when doing any sort of evangelism. Jesus was so adamant that there is only one way to God. We need to have the courage to love others enough to tell them that one church is <u>not as good</u> as another. It can be done—if we love others as Jesus loved us. It takes courage, but it also takes tact when teaching the gospel to others. One way is **NOT** as good as another.

> *A new commandment I give to yo that you love one another: just as I have loved you, you also are to love one another* **(John 13:34)**.

When we act as Jesus did, we will have the strength and love to overcome this evil teachings, which on the surface sound so good...but are so wicked in their fruits. Those fruits are death!!

Chapter Twenty:
Astral Travel

This new-age concept is known by several different names, such as *remote viewing* or *scrying*.

Writings on astral travel have been noted throughout history. In the twenty- first century, classes can be taken on how to achieve it successfully:

In one particular nine-week course offered online, you can learn how to:

- Concentrate and be aware
- Wake up in dreams
- Project into the astral
- Remember your dreams and interpret dream symbols
- Travel in the astral and explore mystical places
- Understand common obstacles when trying to project and how to overcome them
- Protect yourself from negative influences and entities

The course description continues,

> The astral plane is not just a destination, but a whole other dimension of life, which we can use to gain true knowledge about ourselves, our purpose, and about the world and beyond."[6]

One key-point in this presentation is the idea that one should protect oneself from negative influences with such trinkets such as talismans, charms, and spells. People involved in the occult are often the first to warn against its dangers, but they do not realize that all their efforts provide no protection whatsoever against "negative influences." Demonic beings fear only the power of Jesus Christ.

---

[6] More About the Dreams and Out-of-Body Experiences Course," The Gnostic Movement, http://www.gnosticweb.com/node/10081

There are different schools of thought regarding astral travel. Some practitioners subscribe to a theory taught by the 1970 s author and paranormal researcher Robert Monroe, known today as *phasing.* Monroe claimed that the body remains in this dimension, but the spirit can "phase" into a different one. During this phasing, the spirit does not detach completely from the body; it remains linked to it by energy cords that attach to different chakra points. According to Monroe, the astral plane, the universe—all realities exist as individual stops (along with earth) on the long road of consciousness—and human beings can reach these planes of existence with an *energy body.* His work became known for the phrase *out-of-body experience,* also known as *real-time projection.*[7]

A second perspective teaches it is possible for the spirit to detach from the body and visit other dimensions of reality. These realities are separate from the earth, and not subject to its physical laws. Some people compare the detailed facts of astral travel to those found in dreams or visions. Also known as *etheric projection,* a good example of this can be seen in the Hollywood movie *Ghost,* where the main character dies at the beginning of the film and spends the balance of the movie in a transparent type body (etheric body), moving from place to place in the earthly realm.[8]

---

[7] See Monroe Institute history on OBE http://www.monroeinstitute.com/content.phpPsection=Out-of-Body%20 Experiences

[8] Primary source *Kingdom of the Occult* Walter Martin page 313

Chapter Twenty-One:
Astrology

An ancient practice that actual practice is enshrouded in in history. It assumes that the positioning of the stars and planets has a direct influence on people and events. According to this "system," one's lifetime can be plotted and a chart can be made forecasting events of that life-time that are "reliable." A chart that attempts to accomplish this is known as a horoscope.

> For every personal horoscope, the moment of birth is the essential starting point. This, coupled with the latitude and longitude of the individual's birthplace, provides the initial package for the usual astrological chart. While this is elementary, it is not complete; a factor known as "true local time" must also be considered. This "true" time is arrived at by adding or subtracting four minutes for each degree of longitude that your birthplace lies to the east or west of the center of your time zone of birth. Once this has been accomplished, the next step is to convert this "true" time into "sidereal" or star time. This is done with the aid of an ephemeras, a reference book showing the positions of the planets in relationship to the earth. Checking this star time in an astrological table is the last formal move, for in doing so, the theme of the individual's "ascendant"—the astrological sign that is supposed to have been rising on the eastern horizon at the moment of birth —is revealed.[9]

Once you have developed this data — these simple steps are no more difficult than solving a seventh-grade math problem — then you are ready to "chart" your horoscope. This means you align the "ascendant" with the nine-o'clock point on the inner circle of the horoscope, and from there you are prepared to "read" the various zodiacal "houses" that control your life and fortune.[10]

---

[9] "The Soul-Hustlers," by Rene Noorbergen pp.176
[10] How astrologers can justify their practice is explained by Michael Van Buskirk in the same source, pages 178-179

One's future can be forecast, allegedly, because astrology asserts the unity of all things. This is the belief that the Whole (or all of the universe put together) is in some way the same as the Part (or the individual component or man), or that the Part is a smaller reflection of the Whole (macrocosmic/microcosmic model). The position of the planets (the macro) influences and produces a corresponding reaction in man (the micro). This makes a man a pawn in the cosmos with his life and actions pre-determined and unalterable.[11]

It is generally estimated that some forty million Americans have become devotees of astrology. Sometime ago it was estimated that there are supposed to be in our country alone some ten thousand professional astrologers and another 175,000 part-time astrologers. For a fee they will counsel, confide and conjure up a person's future. In the early seventies, it was estimated that astrology had become a $200 million a year business. It is a vast business which seems headed toward a billion-dollar industry per year.

Astrology has made significant inroads into our modern culture within recent years. Its impact on evil may be far more substantial and more lasting than most people realize. Many church members from various religious bodies, who should know better, have fallen victims, not realizing that they are disregarding exceedingly ugly and forth rightly pointed Biblical teaching by manifesting such superstitious regard for the religion of the stars.

There is one thing that is essential to know and to remember when it comes to astrology. Astrology is NOT astronomy. They sound similar but are entirely unrelated. Astrology is not a synonym for astronomy. Astrology is a *RELIGION* of the solar system; whereas, astronomy is a *STUDY of* the solar system. One can be a Christian and be an astronomer. But, I ask you, how could one be a devotee of the principles of astrology and practice New Testament Christianity? Webster defines the two terms of astrology and astronomy in language that reveals their differences. He says that astrology is, "the pseudo -science which treats of the influences of the stars upon human affairs, and of foretelling terrestrial events by their positions and aspects; the divination of the supposed influences of the stars upon human affairs and terrestrial events by their

---

[11] "Astrology, Revival in the Cosmic Garden" page 6.

position and aspects." Webster defines astronomy as, "The science which treats of the celestial bodies, their magnitudes, motions, constitution, etc., a treatise on this science." This universal authority recognizes the differences between the two words. He says that *astrology is a "pseudo-science."* He defines *"pseudo"* as *"Sham; feigned; spurious."* He also recognizes the religious aspects of *astrology* by classifying it as a *"divination."* He says *astronomy* is a *"science."*

Despite claims that astrology is compatible with the Bible, it is not. Beginning with the Old Testament, and especially in the Old Testament, condemnation for the practice of astrology comes from none-other than Almighty God Himself. In Deuteronomy 4:16-19 He says:

> *lest ye corrupt yourselves, and make you a graven image in the form of any figure, the likeness of male or female, the likeness of any beast that is on the earth, the likeness of any winged bird that flieth in the heavens, the likeness of anything that creepeth on the ground, the likeness of any fish that is in the water under the earth; and lest thou lift up thine eyes unto heaven, and when thou seest the sun and the moon and the stars, even all the host of heaven, thou be drawn away and worship them, and serve them, which Jehovah thy God hath allotted unto all the peoples under the whole heaven.*

If we are to worship them, would that not be include being guided by them?

Deuteronomy 18:9-14:

> *When thou art come into the land which Jehovah thy God giveth thee, thou shalt not learn to do after the abominations of those nations. There shall not be found with thee any one that maketh his son or his daughter to pass through the fire, one that useth divination, one that practiseth augury, or an enchanter, or a sorcerer, or a charmer, or a consulter with a familiar spirit, or a wizard, or a necromancer. For whosoever doeth these things is an abomination unto Jehovah: and because of these abominations Jehovah thy God doth drive them out from before thee. Thou shalt be perfect with Jehovah thy God. For these nations, that thou shalt dispossess, hearken*

unto them that practise augury, and unto diviners; but as for thee, Jehovah thy God hath not suffered thee so to do.

Although astronomy is not named in particular, any reference to divination catches astronomy square between the shoulder blades! Next, Isaiah 47:12-15 is a wee-bit clearer on God's feelings.

Stand now with thine enchantments, and with the multitude of thy sorceries, wherein thou hast labored from thy youth; if so be thou shalt be able to profit, if so be thou mayest prevail. Thou art wearied in the multitude of thy counsels: let now the astrologers, the star-gazers, the monthly prognosticators, stand up, and save thee from the things that shall come upon thee. Behold, they shall be as stubble; the fire shall burn them; they shall not deliver themselves from the power of the flame: it shall not be a coal to warm at, nor a fire to sit before. Thus shall the things be unto thee wherein thou hast labored: they that have trafficked with thee from thy youth shall wander everyone to his quarter; there shall be none to save thee.

Jeremiah 10:1-5:

Hear ye the word which Jehovah speaketh unto you, O house of Israel: thus saith Jehovah, Learn not the way of the nations, and be not dismayed at the signs of heaven; for the nations are dismayed at them. For the customs of the peoples are vanity; for one cutteth a tree out of the forest, the work of the hands of the workman with the axe. They deck it with silver and with gold; they fasten it with nails and with hammers, that it move not. They are like a palm-tree, of turned work, and speak not: they must needs be borne, because they cannot go. Be not afraid of them; for they cannot do evil, neither is it in them to do good.

Now, we turn to the pages of the New Testament. We read in Acts 7:42-43:

But God turned, and gave them up to serve the host of heaven; as it is written in the book of the prophets, Did ye offer unto me slain beasts and sacrifices Forty years in the wilderness, O house of Israel? And ye took up the tabernacle of Moloch, And the star of the god Rephan, The figures which ye made to worship them: And I will carry you away beyond Babylon.

Generally speaking, God need only condemn something once but here, how many times was it? We who seek to do God's will ought to be happy with what we have seen. Astrology is man-made, and it has the condemnation of our Creator.

Chapter Twenty-Two:
Automatic Writing

Automatic writing is a feature of the occult practice of communicating "with the dead." (which is, in reality, communicating with evil spirits since the dead are unable to commune with the living. Examples will follow hereafter under the heading "Communicating with the Dead.")

History

The earliest reference to automatic writing was from the 16th century when men named John Dee, and Edward Kelley received communication from the "Enochian Angels," which became a vital part of "Enochian magic." The language and grammar were said to be very complex. Dee also claimed that the Enochian instruction included information regarding the elixir of life in the ruins of Glastonbury Abbey

Parapsychologist William Fletcher Barrett wrote that "automatic messages may take place either by the writer passively holding a pencil on a sheet of paper, or by the planchette or by an 'ouija board'. In spiritualism, spirits are claimed to take control of the hand of a medium to write messages, letters, and even entire books. Automatic writing can happen in a trance or waking state. The Surrealist poet Robert Desnos claimed he was among the most gifted in automatic writing. Some psychical researchers such as Thomson Jay Hudson have alleged no spirits are involved in automatic writing, and the subconscious mind is the explanation.

Shortly after his 1917 marriage to Georgie Hyde-Lees the poet W. B. Yeats came to be heavily influenced by her delving into what they referred to as "the automatic script."

The medium Pierre L. O. A. Keeler had an alleged spirit writing communication from Abraham Lincoln currently exhibited at the Lily Dale Museum. Despite Lincoln being a well-known skeptic and Keeler having been known to employ magician's tricks. This is used as one of the many examples of skeptics purportedly endorsing spiritualism.

A prominent alleged example of automatic writing is the Brattleboro hoax. When Charles Dickens died in 1870, he left The Mystery of Edwin Drood unfinished. According to the itinerant printer T.P. James this angered Dickens' spirit so much that he channeled the rest of the novel through James's hand. This is supposed to have begun on Christmas Eve 1872 and continued in thrice weekly sessions until completion.[12]

Skeptics

According to skeptical investigator Joe Nickell, "automatic writing is produced while one is in a dissociated state. It is a form of motor automatism, or unconscious muscular activity as this case indicates, many attribute automatic writing to spirits or other entities. In one famous instance, Pearl Lenore Curran of St. Louis discovered in 1913 that she was taking dictation from a spirit. As her Ouija board's pointer spelled out: "Many moons ago I lived. Again, I come—Patience Worth, my name." Curran soon found that "Patience" could communicate by speaking through Curran's voice or by controlling her fingers as she typed. Alas, however, there was no evidence to confirm Patience's claim that she was born in England in 1649 or that, at age forty-five, she was killed in America by Indians. Investigator Milbourne Christopher concluded that Curran had "discovered not a spirit but a way to express herself."[13]

Automatic writing is produced while one is in a dissociated state. It is a form of *motor automatism*, or unconscious muscular activity, the cause not only of Ouija-board planchette movement but also of such phenomena as table tipping, "trance" painting or music composition, dowsing, and so on. It is also responsible for some impulsive acts.[14] (A second category, sensory automatism, includes apparitions, dreams, hallucinations, specific inspirations, etc.)[15]

So, as you can tell, the jury is still out on the psychic phenomena known as automatic writing. There are strong witnesses for both

---

[12] Paul Heller-Dickens in the Spirit World. The Rutland Herald 4/25/18

[13] P. 129

[14] A Case of Automatic Writing From Robert G. Ingersoll's Spirit?

[15] See Guiley (1991), pp.45-48; Gardner (1957), p. 109.

sides of the fence on this matter. It is to be noted that automatic writing almost always follows the use of the Ouija board and its activities.

If in fact, it is truly a psychic occurrence, then there are a lot of untrue spirits because of scripture—one simple verse—spells the end of the deceased communicants. In the book of Hebrews, Chapter 9, verse 27 is short and concise. It says:

And inasmuch as it is appointed unto men once to die, and after this cometh judgment.

That is it, when the word of God means something once it is like it is shouted from the mountaintops. Well, we've been told that man dies once and then the judgment. Are souls able to travel far and wide doing whatever they want? You die once and then comes judgment. Short and sweet. Since it isn't humans talking and writing on the Ouija board or using automatic writing, that leaves only one possibility—evil spirit. Are you wanting them to communicate through you? Not me, thank you very much.

Chapter Twenty-Three:
Communicating with the Dead

The Threefold makeup of man.

When it comes to the subject of communicating with the dead, there are great numbers of things that need to be discussed before the topic can be answered. So, let's begin with a few short facts from which our conclusions can be drawn.

The first is that we consist of a triune nature. This means that man exists in three parts. The first is that we consist of a body, a soul, and a spirit. The body is the outward part of our make-up. Scriptures such as Romans 6:12; 2 Corinthians 4:11 and 16; 5:1 talk about our fleshly part only. Paul then relates in 5:23:

> *And the God of peace himself sanctify you wholly; and may your spirit and soul and body be preserved entire, without blame at the coming of our Lord Jesus Christ. Then Hebrews 4:12 says: For the word of God is living, and active, and sharper than any two-edged sword, and piercing even to the dividing of soul and spirit, of both joints and marrow*

This speaks of the dividing of soul and spirit showing them to be different.

What Happens at Death

What happens to the body at death? Do the soul and spirit exist after death? Once the body dies, what becomes of the other two components? Well, Ecclesiastes 12:7 tells us:

> *and the dust returneth to the earth as it was, and the spirit returneth unto God who gave it.*

The body returns to the dust from which it is composed, but the spirit goes back to God. Thankfully, Jesus Christ fills in the rest of the puzzle pieces with his discourse on Luke 16:19-31: (note that it **nowhere** says that it is a parable—as some will say; and that even if it is one, Jesus never gave a parable about something that didn't or couldn't happen).

> *Now there was a certain rich man, and he was clothed in purple and fine linen, faring sumptuously every day: and a certain beggar named Lazarus was laid at his gate, full of sores, and desiring to be fed with the crumbs that fell from the rich man's table; yea, even the dogs came and licked his sores. And it came to pass, that the beggar died, and that he was carried away by the angels into Abraham's bosom: and the rich man also died, and was buried. And in Hades, he lifted up his eyes, being in torments, and seeth Abraham afar off, and Lazarus in his bosom. And he cried and said, Father Abraham, have mercy on me, and send Lazarus, that he may dip the tip of his finger in water, and cool my tongue; for I am in anguish in this flame. But Abraham said, Son, remember that thou in thy lifetime receivedst thy good things, and Lazarus in like manner evil things: but now here he is comforted, and thou art in anguish. And besides all this, between us and you there is a great gulf fixed, that they that would pass from hence to you may not be able, and that none may cross over from thence to us. And he said, I pray thee therefore, father, that thou wouldest send him to my father's house; for I have five brethren; that he may testify unto them, lest they also come into this place of torment. But Abraham saith, They have Moses and the prophets; let them hear them. And he said, Nay, father Abraham: but if one goes to them from the dead, they will repent. And he said unto him, If they hear not Moses and the prophets, neither will they be persuaded if one rise from the dead.*

A quick familiarization: Two men, a rich man, and a poor man, live their lives, and both die. Notice that they are awake and are aware that one is in paradise (known as Abraham's Bosom) and the other in torment—in flames. They cannot get from where they are because a great "gulf" is fixed between them that they cannot cross. The rich man is in torment in flames but tries to get Abraham to send someone to warn his brothers so that they don't end up there!

Now, having looked at this lesson that Jesus taught, we can draw some conclusions: First, according to this story that Jesus taught, when we die, we go straight to either paradise or torment. No trip to go, no $200 or wandering around anywhere. Next, we can want to send someone back "to warn" our friends and neighbors, but that isn't allowed.

Finally one last bit of cream on top of the cake: Ecclesiastes 9:4-5:

> *For to him that is joined with all the living there is hope; for a living dog is better than a dead lion. For the living know that they shall die: but the dead know not anything, neither have they any more a reward; for the memory of them is forgotten.*

The dead know not anything so with what do they use to maintain conversations with all of the living who are seeking for "righteousness" with those using the Ouija boards and automatic writers that we hear from so often?

Conclusions Drawn

Since we have eliminated the dead as a source of contact, what is left to pick? There can be one of two possible causes. One is fraud or chicaner, and the other one would be evil spirits. The spirits were cast out along with Satan when they started a war in heaven at some point in the past. There cannot be any rock-solid proof, but my bet would be with the second choice. Having experienced that connection, I would say that they are behind all of the mischief and downright evil in the world today. Another vital means of communication is in regards to spiritism, mediums, channeling, and seances. Those will be covered in their articles.

Chapter Twenty-Four:
Differing Dimensions

We know that our earth is one dimension of which the Bible speaks. It is this physical world that allows our birth, life and ultimately our physical death which leads our souls into the next. There is another one very apparent, and that is Heaven, where God has his throne. It was bridged when God sent His son Jesus Christ to come and rescue us from our sins. Because of that gracious and loving act, we now have access to this realm of infinite power, indescribable love, and cosmic justice. There also seems to be a separate realm of darkness where Satan has his rule but also has access to the earth-realm. It seems to be where the battles wage rather than in heaven. Satan and his forces were cast down when there was war in heaven at some time in the past. That phase of the war ended in the defeat of evil in heaven.

There is another place, referred to as "the Hadean realm" where the souls go after the physical separation of soul, spirit, and body when we die. I am not quite sure how to label it except by how Jesus referred to it in Luke 16:19-31. There we see that Hades is where we go at death, to one of two places: the righteous to paradise and the wicked to torment. Whether this is another dimension or not is a question. It seems to be a holding place for all people until the fullness of humanity is achieved. Then comes judgement leading to either Heaven or Hell.

The last dimension seems to be described by the condition of its occupants where they are seen as "wandering stars for whom is reserved the blackness of darkness is reserved forever." (Jude 13) This third spiritual realm is composed of spiritual darkness, which is disconnected from the creator. It is prevailed upon by the "prince of the powers of the air," the "spirit that worketh in the sons of disobedience. (Eph. 2:2) This is a place that is described as "outer darkness" (Matt. 8:12, 22:13, 25:30) "suffering." (Jude 7), "prison" (1 Peter 3:19). Peter indicated that there were some who already chained in darkness, awaiting judgment. This is one place where we don't want to end up. Let us work righteousness that our fate would be far different than those already there.

Chapter Twenty-Five:
Electronic Voice Phenomena

The phrase "Electronic Voice Phenomena" has been made to be greatly followed by those who are alleged "ghost hunters." all across the scene up to those who refer to themselves as "Parapsychologists." This is entirely from the left to the right as it is a "hot" word as well as a very interesting topic to those who are denizens of this world and its religio-political systems. It received its greatest boost when it first appeared on the Sci-Fi Network television program called **"Ghost Hunters."** It was used extensively by staff as well as guests who swore that it was authentic and practiced it every week at one time or another. Now, not claiming either its truth or its fallacy, it is known that if someone makes enough claims that something is true that after enough claims, people begin to accept it as the truth. That seems to be the case for EVP.

History

As the Spiritualist religious movement came into popularity, people began to believe that the spirits of the dead could be contacted by those referred to as "mediums." Also, belief became widespread that the spirits could be reached by some of the new technologies such as photography and eventually the gramophone and sound recording machines. In a *Scientific American* interview, Thomas Edison commented on the possibility of recording, and maybe even that contact could be made with those in the spiritual realm. He stated that if the spirits were capable of subtle influences that perhaps a recording could be made of it. Now, following his history, we do know that he did hot succeed in producing such an appliance, but others did. Although Spiritualism declined in the 20th century under the guidance of magicians such as Houdini and later James Randi. Their efforts to uncover the charlatans did a lot of damage to the cause, and a great many were exposed as frauds. Despite the setbacks, experimentation with various devices continued with some success in recording different events were touted as complete successes.[16]

---

[16] Adapted from the Wikipedia article, *Electronic Voice Phenomena*.

Fact or Fallacy?

People who are Pro-EVP consider EVP to be a form of paranormal phenomena in which words and phrases are to be found in recordings made from old-fashioned cassette players up to today's complicated digital voice recorders. The words and phrases can be heard through the static, often, being perceived as answers to questions. Now, not meaning to interject my own experiences into the discussion, but I have a rather memorable EVP experience which I will relate. When we were in the occult, we were very interested in EVPs and took a cassette player with a new blank tape and began asking it questions. After about 5 minutes of mumbling, quiet answers, I was a little irritated and said, "Is there anyone there?" and waited about 30 seconds. There was, in fact, an obvious answer that I will never forget till the end of my days. There was not a whisper, or a hiss or pop but a very clear, deep baritone voice which very clearly, concisely said: "Yes, I am here." It scared us so bad that we never did an EVP again. It was blood-running-cold, terrorizing in nature. So, you can see on which side of the argument I stand. I genuinely wish that, like all of my occult experiences, that this did not happen, but it did, so perhaps you can learn from my mistakes!

Scientists have varying degrees of belief or disbelief on the subject of EVP. Some regard EVP as a form of auditory pareidolia (interpreting random sounds as voices in one's language) and a pseudoscience promulgated by popular culture. Prosaic explanations for EVP include apophenia (perceiving patterns in random information), equipment artifacts, and hoaxes. They especially thrive in the "hoax" department.

There have been articles such as "Communicating with the Dead," which give a much longer explanation, but for safety's sake, I will restate the facts as they relate to EVPs.

The general idea behind EVPs is that you are communicating with the dead. I used Jesus's lesson in Luke 16:19-31(see that chapter for the scriptures laid out) where Jesus in effect says that when one dies, he goes to either paradise or torment and that there is no returning to life as we knew it and no one can communicate with those living. Also, Ecclesiastes 9:4-5 which says that those who are dead know not anything. These two sets of verses teach us that if we are speaking to or hearing someone that that individual is not a human being but in effect, a demon or the head of all evil, Satan. That ought to allow you to study God's word and arm yourselves with the Sword of the Spirit. Not to aimlessly repeat, but God's Word is a weapon of unimaginable power and effectiveness. I knew that writing a book of this type was going to put a big target in the middle of my back. Quite the opposite occurred. Knowing God's Word and using it offensively is quite a fantastic experience. The verse that gave me the title for this book has explained this very well. 2 Cor. 10:4-6 says:

> *(for the weapons of our warfare are not of the flesh, but mighty before God to the* **casting down of strongholds**)*, casting down imaginations, and every high thing that is exalted against the knowledge of God, and bringing every thought into captivity to the obedience of Christ; and being in readiness to avenge all disobedience, when your obedience shall be made full.*

Chapter Twenty-Six:
Fortunetelling

To define fortunetelling is very difficult but I will try: Fortunetelling is the "art" of forecasting the future supposedly by supernatural sources. It is an ancient practice which is still practiced today. Another name for it is divination. One who practices this practice is known as a diviner. A diviner uses various methods to receive his "knowledge" such as psychometry, palmistry, cartomancy, and something known as mirror-mantic. These all, or one, can be used to arrive at a knowledge of the future, another term that can and should be used is something known as "a guess."

> . . . People infected or burdened by fortunetelling and occult phenomena very frequently suffer in the following ways:
>
> The characters of such people reveal abnormal passions, instability, violent tempers, addiction to alcohol, nicotine and sexual vices, selfishness, gossiping, egotism, cursing, etc.
>
> Their religious lives reveal on the one hand an antagonism toward religion, callousness, skepticism, a vicious critical attitude and an inability to pray or read the Bible if they are an atheistic type of person, while on the other hand, the pious type reveals a self-righteousness, a spiritual pride, phariseeism, hypocrisy and an insensitivity to the workings of the Holy Spirit.
>
> Medically speaking the families of those involved in fortunetelling reveal in a remarkable way such things as nervous disturbances, psychopathic and hysteric symptoms, cases of St. Vitus' dance, symptoms of paralysis, epileptics, freaks, deaf-mutes, cases of mediumistic psychoses, and a general tendency toward emotional and mental illnesses, etc.[17]

---

[17] Kurt Koch, *Between Christ and Satan,* Grand Rapids, MI: Kregel Publications, 1968, pp. 49, 50.

Danny Korem lists specific techniques used by a fortuneteller, which give realism to their readings:

(1) Observation of sensory clues.

(2) Prior knowledge of the subject obtained secretly before reading.

(3) Ability to think on one's feet and change the direction of the reading without hesitation or detection.

(4) Understanding of human nature.

(5) Utilization of the cards or any other apparatus to pick up sensory clues or change the direction of the reading when off the track.

(6) An element of luck and a keen sense of playing the odds so that a well-placed guess may produce spectacular results.[18]

The debate never comes to an end whether fortunetelling is just a glorified con game or not. What does not come up for debate is that ALL forms of fortunetelling a.k.a. Divination is an abomination in God's sight. He says it, makes it very clear and expects that we should obey his command on it.

> ***Deuteronomy 18:10-12*** *There shall not be found with thee any one that maketh his son or his daughter to pass through the fire, one that <u>useth divination</u>, one that practiseth augury, or an enchanter, or a sorcerer, or a charmer, or a consuler with a familiar spirit, or a wizard, or a necromancer. For whosoever doeth these things is an abomination unto Jehovah: and because of these abominations, Jehovah thy God doth drive them out from before thee.*

Some would insist that God had given the fortunetellers their ability. This could not be so since God has forbidden it in his word.

There is room left for some descriptions of the various forms of divination used in fortunetelling:

---

[18] Danny Korem and Paul Meier, *The Fakers,* Grand Rapids, MI: Baker Book House, 1980, p. 107

Psychometry—this consists in the fortuneteller holding an item belonging to the "readee" and venturing with a large number of guesses supposedly based upon the physic materials left on that object.

Palmistry-Fortune being told based upon the lines on hands as well as left, type and a myriad of other supposed biometric information being deposited there. Again, guesses.

Cartomancy is the use of the Tarot Cards. See article on **Tarot Cards**

Mirror-Mantic—the use of crystal balls, mirrors, rock crystals, or still water as mirrors of the future. This is an ancient method of divination. The one staring into the mirror is supposed to reach a state of clairvoyance where future events can be seen, thus allowing him access to the future.

The plain and simple fact is that we do not need these "services" if we have the Holy Spirit indwelling us.

Other Types of Fortunetelling[19]

Teacup Reading—This form of divination interprets the shapes and relative positions left by tea leaves at the bottom of a cup. Fortunes are told using one same principle as are found in the oriental I CHING readings.

Geomancy—This system of divination employs a map with 12 divisions which the symbols of geomancy are placed in conjunction with the plane

Pyromancy—Divination by use of fire configurations.

Aeromancy—This form of divination observes atmospheric conditions or lies on the surface of an open body of water.

Arithmancy—Divination by numbers, especially by attaching mystic significance to the numbers associated with a person, especially those numbers associated with the letters of the person's name.

Augury—"In ancient Rome, divination by the flight of birds. The word is us generally for all kinds of divination, also for any omen or sign on which divination is or can be based" (Frank Gaynor, op. cit., p. 21).

---

[19] These are taken from *Understanding the Occult* by Josh McDowell, p. 195.

Capnomancy—This form of divination uses the smoke of an altar or sacrifice incense as a means of foretelling the future.

Rhapsodomancy—This form of divination is based upon a line in a sacred book that strikes the eye when the book is opened after the diviner prays, meditates or invokes the help of spirits.

In conclusion, there are many different names for fortunetellers, mediums. By whatever name, they are entirely condemned by the Bible. God calls them detestable in Deuteronomy 18:11-12. One who practices such things was sentenced to death under the Old Testament theocracy (Leviticus 20:6, 27).

Such false prophets (Jeremiah 14:14) were sometimes called astrologers: (Isaiah 47:13), mediums (Deuteronomy 18:11), diviners (Deuteronomy 18:14), magicians (Genesis 41:8), soothsayers (Isaiah 2:6), sorcerers (Acl 13: 6, 8), and spiritists (Deuteronomy 18:11).

The Lord God promises that someday he will "cut off sorceries from your hand, and you will have fortunetellers no more" (Micah 5:12)

Chapter Twenty-Seven:
I-Ching

The I Ching (pronounced *Yee Jing*) is an ancient tool (initially with yarrow sticks) used in Chinese divination. Today, three coins are tossed, and their pattern recorded to produce answers to personal questions. Attributed to the great Chinese emperor Fu Hsi (2850 BC), the I Ching is thought to have developed in meaning and structure over a period of a thousand years under the influence of King Wen (founder of the Chou Dynasty in 1150 BC) and finally, under the revered philosopher Confucius (550 BC). It was after the contributions of Confucius that the I Ching came to be known as *The Book of Changes.* Today, the I Ching, also known as *The Oracle of Changes,* is viewed as fulfilling "at least two functions: book of wisdom, and oracular book."

Book of wisdom—because it inspired the Chinese way of thinking and generally the whole Chinese culture, being at the same time a Ting (ritual vase) in which these currents mingled.

Oracular book—because it can be used as means of investigation and foretelling success or failure.

The book of wisdom distinguishes itself through the educational passages—undoubtedly written by Confucius' advocates and legists from whom we can quote an example at random. For many people, the book is a useful manners handbook or book of cultivating the noble man; a character called to play an active part in social and political state life (from here derives Confucius' influence).

The oracular book uses the 64 hexagrams as a landmark of orientation regarding the evolution of the present events. Each hexagram describes a typical situation and is accompanied by an oracular indication of the kind: "good fortune," "misfortune," "remorse," "humiliation." Several typical situations may be found here along with their indications, that is, the advice to be followed in the given circumstances.

Developed on the Chinese belief that all life is subject to either chaos or order (yin and yang), the I Ching uses a system of coin tossing and sixty-four hexagrams to predict the future and offer advice on life choices in response to direct questions. Yin is the dark element; it represents multiple aspects such as the feminine/sadness/night and is symbolized by earth and water. Yang is the light element; it represents the masculine/joyful/day. These two elements embody the principle of yin and yang; they are in constant motion—moving and changing like currents in the ocean of life—and they influence every aspect of existence.

I Ching more than likely was influenced by the ancient Chinese religion of Taoism (founded by Lao Tzu in 550 BC), which teaches there is no personal god, only an impersonal supreme force called the *Tao.* Good and evil are opposite but complementary forces, and the goal of humanity should be to become free of selfish desires, to flow freely with the Tao.

Taijitu symbol represents the principle of yin and yang.

Often referred to as the *Oracle,* I Ching was consulted for everything from military decisions to investments, marriage, and children—and it is still consulted today. It is a complex numerical and philosophic divination tool, and as such has not achieved the worldwide popularity of a simpler device, such as the Ouija board.[20]

---

[20] Martin, p. 327.

Chapter Twenty-Eight: Magic

This magic is not the type which is seen today as an illusionary form of entertainment loved by millions and is a multimillion-dollar industry seen across the nation by millions of followers. We also speak of "magic being in the air" on special events. That is not the type of magic to which we refer.

Magic, which happens to be mainly used by witches can be seen as thus:

Black Magic

For some who practice witchcraft, magic is viewed as something supernatural and seen as something which they can access to achieve personal gains, success against enemies, etc. Its characters involve specialized spiritual agencies which happen to be outside the natural rhythm of things. These things would be seen as demons or elementals. These are outside the natural order and because of that cannot be studied with any hope of empirical science or scholars. These are not according to natural laws and will, in most cases, contradict natural laws. This is the realm of the witch and her tool, Black magic. In this, supernatural agencies are invoked, and these end up being beyond natural explanation.

White Magic

To understand black magic as much as we are able, we need to know a little about its polar opposite (according to witchcraft sources), white magic.

White magic is claimed to be the use of magical powers and abilities in an unselfish manner for the benefit of others. Some believe that a person can be cured of bewitchment (a curse being placed upon them through black magic) by white magic. The point being missed here is that all forms of witchcraft are under God's curse so white, black, maybe even purple (kidding kdf) magic is forbidden. Although white magic was and is used to combat evil, it still comes from an ungodly source and should not be practiced in any form.

Sympathetic Magic

Briefly looking at a few other forms helps us to zero in on just what exactly constitutes as "Black Magic."

Sympathetic magic is control of a person, animal, situation or hopefully, outcome by the principle that "like produces like." Things having a resemblance to each other in shape have magical relationships. As an example, a drawing of a deer pierced by arrows supposedly would assist the hunters of a tribe in accomplishing the same thing, piercing a deer through with arrows. It is a very primitive sort of magic practiced by those in primitive, or harsh, situations to achieve the objective, whatever it might be.

Lycanthropy

Lycanthropy is a form of magic in which belief is held that human beings, under certain circumstances and conditions, can change into the form of animals. This "magic" is a held idea among those who believe in "shapeshifting," which is just another form of lycanthropy exercised among more modern-day practitioners of this form of magic.

Although lycanthropy is considered mere legend and superstition, modern reports of this occurring have been reported.

Summary View of the Two Main Types of Magic

These various (and these are only a very few descriptions) types of magic have led to occultists making a distinction between so-called white and black magic. Part of this comes from a witch's relation to "Christianity." To those who are pure Satanist, black magic is the "flavor of the day" while supposed Christian-influenced witch, white magic is their "cup of tea—or roots, herbs, etc." The Satanist supposedly draws their power from the spirits of the dark side and kingdom of darkness. Because of the stereotype of the witch as Satanist, those adhering to Christianity in whatever warped form began referring to themselves as "White Witches" and began referring to their magic as beneficial. Ultimately, the "white" or "black" related to pure intentions and not as moral grounding. God says in **Deuteronomy 18:9-12:**

When thou art come into the land which Jehovah thy God giveth thee, thou shalt not learn to do after the abominations of those nations. There shall not be found with thee any one that maketh his son or his daughter to pass through the fire, one that useth divination, one that practiseth augury, or an enchanter, or a sorcerer, or a charmer, or a consulter with a familiar spirit, or a wizard, or a necromancer. For whosoever doeth these things is an abomination unto Jehovah: and because of these abominations, Jehovah thy God doth drive them out from before thee.

Chapter Twenty-Nine:
Mediums and Channeling

In the later years of the twentieth century, the term "mediumship" and "channeling" have become very popular with the general public. All facets of the occult have grown tremendously just as interest in organized religion has declined in the same way the occult has grown. Faith in religion has declined over the years. People are casting their faith from themselves so that they can believe in parlor tricks and lying wonders.

The term "Mediumship" has become popular, and a lot of people are seeking this supposed "honor" in droves. The definition of a medium is:

> The process whereby a human instrument, known as a MEDIUM or CHANNEL, is used by one or more discarnate, spirit personalities for the purpose(s) of presenting information, verifiable or otherwise; causing so-called paranormal activities to occur; channeling forth certain types of energies; manifesting themselves for objective examination and/or identification. From this definition, we see the following: mediumship involves a cooperating effort between a person on the Earth plane (the medium or channel) and a person in Spirit (the communicator). There are several objectives behind the manifestation of mediumship. In addition to this, we see that mediumship is used by those in Spirit for the following purposes: to present information, which may or may not be verifiable; to cause certain types of paranormal activities to occur; to channel forth certain types of energies; to manifest themselves materially. Thus, mediumship can be distinguished as two basic types: mental mediumship; physical mediumship. Mental mediumship involves the relating of information, through communication, via the varied aspects of thought transference, or mental telepathy. Telepathy is the relaying of information via thought, without using any of the five physical senses . . . Physical mediumship involves the manipulation and trans-

155

formation of physical systems and energies. The spirit operators, in this case, are causing something to happen upon the Earth plane. What it is that happens varies with the style of mediumship involved, but the results can be seen and heard by others" ("Medium").

Apport: This is the materializing of objects during a seance. Any good magician can duplicate such.

Clairvoyance: The supposed (pretended) ability to see things without the use of the physical senses.

Clairaudience: The supposed (pretended) ability to hear things without the use of the physical senses.

Telekinesis: The supposed (pretended) ability to move things with the power of the mind.

Psychokinesis: The supposed (pretended) production of things by the power of the mind.

Spiritualism: The belief that the personality lives on after death and can communicate in various ways with the living, usually through someone called a medium or a channeler.

Seance: A meeting of spiritualists to bring up departed spirits for communicating with them. This may be done by the medium or channeler speaking in a strange voice claiming to be the voice of the departed spirit. It used to be common to have physical manifestations (by trickery) of figures, raps, or tables levitating.[21] ()

History

How did spiritualism and belief in mediums and channelers get started? Believe or not, it all started with a prank by pre-teenage girls, Margaret, and Kate Fox, March 31, 1848, (the day before April Fool's Day). This took place in Hydesville, New York, about 20 miles from Rochester. This prank was so exploited by their sister, Mrs. Daniel Underhill (then Mrs. Fish) who was much older than they, that for years afterward, they traveled the great cities of

---

[21] First Spiritual Temple, a Spiritualist Church.
http://www.fst.org/medium.htm

the world as genuine mediums. The spiritualist churches, first formed by their older sister, and the movement of today, traces its origins to them and still hails them as genuine.

Mediums have been around for a very long time and were especially "potent" throughout the 1800 s and up until the time of the legendary Harry Houdini who devoted a significant amount of time and effort to prove that these supposed mediums/channels were nothing short of downright con-men and frauds. His time was divided between his magic and hunting down con-men equally. Today the job is underway by a gentleman named James Randi, who, like Houdini, is a magician and exposer of frauds.

The best known channeler of this generation is a man named James Van Praagh. He has been on many television shows and has a three-year backlog of paying customers.
The Skeptics Dictionary has this to say in its article on James Van Praagh:

> "He plays a kind of twenty-questions game with his audience. He goes fishing, rapidly casting his baited questions one after the other until he gets a bite. Then he reels the fish in. Sometimes he falters, but most of the fish don't get away. He just re-baits and goes after the fish again until he re-hooks. The fish love it. When he can't get a good bite, he reminds his audience that sometimes the message is in fragments, sometimes he doesn't understand it, sometimes he misinterprets it, etc. If he's wrong, don't blame him since he never claimed to be perfect. . . What saves him much of the time are ambiguous questions that end with "am I right?" and the client saying "yes," though we have no idea what the "yes" is in response to. Is he sincere in what he does? Is he self-deceived, or is he a deceiver?"

Listen to what the experts have to say:

> "I contacted numerous mentalists [magicians who specialize in mindreading tricks-D.C.] about Van Praagh, and they all assure me, without reservation, that it would be impossible for him to be self-deceiving because these are techniques that they all use and do so consciously and purposefully. I was told that I was naive in trying to give Van

157

Praagh the benefit of the doubt. I even talked to someone I know who works a 900-psychic hotline, who is a skeptic but believes there might be somethings to "some" psychic abilities. It turns out he knows James Van Praagh and many of the people who work with him in that industry . . . And he assures me that Van Praagh is not self-deceived. The psychic industry consensus, this source tells me, is that James Van Praagh knows exactly what he is doing"[22]

So, there you have it. Mediums and channels have been proven to be false by such luminaries as Harry Houdini up until the present day. James Randi has offered a phenomenal amount of money to any scientifically proven medium/channeler and had something like 80+ people try for the money only to be proven as charlatans and fakes. If there is a real medium out there, they can make a lot of money for very little work....

---

[22] http://www.holysmoke.org/skeptictank.praagh.htm

Chapter Thirty:
Numerology

Numerology has a mysterious beginning. Some claim that it comes down to us from ancient Babylon while still others give it a recent onset. Either way, it has had a great influence or the leaders and peoples of the world.

Modern numerology claims great age and claims that it has metaphysical abilities based upon number analysis based upon some very basic information like birth date and name.

During the Talmudic and Mishnaic period, some began to believe that in addition to the literal meaning, there was a symbolic meaning from that which could be drawn. They felt that there were deep divine mysteries associated with certain letters and names of places. Also, historical accounts such as that of Jacob and Esau, Hagar and Rahab were much, much more than mere history. Therefore, little historical meaning was sought while they tried to learn the mysteries of God using various systems of exegesis. The biggie among these was gematria, which is the study of letters.

Today, there are those who continue their study of the Bible only in the sense of individual letters and their relationship to those around, both near and far.

Numerology has morphed itself into a system of occult divination where all sorts of charting can be done using names, dates, and all orders of numbers. Fans of this "method" exalt in how many charts that be generated by adherents of this pseudo-system of divination. Despite all of this the Pythagorean tenet that *all is number* is still very present. The whole edifice is still built on this foundation.

This is quite different from the meaning of symbolic numbers used in the Hebrew and Greek cultures of the Bible. Some biblical numbers follow a significant pattern as used by God and His people, but these are never used to forecast the future. Therefore, the meanings behind numerics in the Bible cannot be carried to an extreme to hunt for knowledge not present. Absent from all biblical context is the occultic belief that numbers influence people's lives.

The Following Interesting description comes from James Randi's "An Encyclopedia of Claims, Frauds, and Hoaxes of the Occult and Supernatural " and gives a little humorous food for thought:

> **Numerology, The mystical attraction of necessary qualities of numbers**, resulted in strange theories about magical powers that could be invoked or discovered by carrying out certain arithmetical operations. Such a belief, based on an idea of Pythagoras that all facts can be reduced to numbers, results from a failure to understand the true nature of the concept of number.
>
> In applying numerology to a person's name, for example, there are many different systems in this "art" for assigning numbers to the letters of the alphabet, adding them up and arriving at a series of qualities, characteristics, and specific facts that are said to apply to that person. The dubious nature of the practice becomes obvious.
>
> Three of the most popular systems among many, many such systems to determine "name numbers are shown here:

A = 1	1	1
B =2	5	2
C =3	6	3
D = 4	9	4
E =5	3	5
F =8	8	6
G = 3	8	7
H = 5	3	8
I = 1	9	9

The third column of numbers represents what is known as the Pythagorean system. All of these systems require the user to add together each of the digits representing each letter in the name, then to add the digits of the resulting number, and repeat that process until a number less than ten has been arrived at. This final digit is interpreted according to the following table:

1. action, aggression, ambition, leadership, purpose

2. balance, passivity, receptivity

3. brilliance, gaiety, versatility

4. dullness, endurance, steadiness

5. adventure, instability, sexuality

6. dependability, domesticity, harmony

7. knowledge, mystery, solitariness

8. material success, worldly involvement

9. great achievement, inspiration, spirituality

It can be seen that there is no standard and no consistency in numerology—let alone rationality— but it provides a secure method for the naive person to play a satisfying game without having to apply any intellectual powers to the matter.

Gematria is a form of numerology which employs the Hebrew alphabet, in which all the letters also have numerical values.

Modern numerologists, quick to adopt new technologies to prove and enlarge old claptrap, have now turned to a computer number system, the American Standard for Coded Interchange of Information (ASCII), for the further deep meaning of the alphabet.

Chapter Thirty-One:
Palmistry

Palmistry is also known as chiromancy and is a very, very old form of divination. It is most well-known of all the types of the occult form of divination. In it, the hand is studied for the length of lines and how they interplay with each other, indicating the future extent of life and so forth. There have been many famous "chiromancers" over the centuries who have become supposed experts on the topics and who have taught different doctrines as to what is to be looked at, how long the lines are and the interplay of these lines showing the length of life etc.

As my form of reference, I will be quoting "The Encyclopedia of Occult Sciences," which is supposed to be an expert on these many topics. It was dated 1939-1968.

It begins with the types of hands-pointed, square, conical, and spatulate. Each is supposed to indicate personality and some indication of the length of life. Every finger, joint, and section between joints are named and supposedly have their functions. As a quick example of what I am speaking, the first section of the index finger being longer in length indicates "pride and obstinacy." If that first joint is "long and strong," it means "strong-will power." First joint "ball-shaped," that indicates "pigheadedness, even brutishness." Enough for picking on that poor particular joint.

Each finger and its physical characteristics are discussed at length. A good example of this is the pronouncement that a thumb which is bent backward is indicative of "cowardice, moral weakness, and fear." A long middle finger is a gloomy pride, doubt of self, fatalism. A short ring finger is "indifference to glory, and if very short, low instincts."

The handshake has obvious implications that I will try to list without over-doing it. *Ordinary with good-nature-*Superficial or cunning men. *Short*-Men avaricious, *Drag-*

ging-The simple formality of the indifferent. *Brutal*-That of a bully or rude man.

Broad and Frank-Of a friend, a good-hearted man. *Heavy*-Of the indolent to whom all movement is a task. *From the tips of the fingers*-Of the disdainful (insolent gesture) *Caressing and lasting*-Of a voluptuary, *Caressing* with pressure-Carnal desire.

The lines of the hand are the great revealers, the "pythonesses" who are easily questioned and who respond most obediently. They indicate vitality, energy, and sensitiveness which are assigned from the time of birth on. They supposedly reflect the will of the brain, impulses, starts, weaknesses, and the whole of the past.

The lines of the hand are supposedly formed in the womb at the same time as the face is formed. "God placed signs in the hands of men," says some alleged sacred book. I can't find that in the Bible, so it is someone's idea of truth. The diversity of temperaments and vitalities causes their variety. Like the fingerprint, there are no two individuals with the same lines. The more lines we have, the more sensitive is the soul. Those who work the soil or simple jobs have far fewer lines than are those with more complicated occupations. Each hand corresponds to the opposite side of the brain, the right hand to the left hemisphere and vice versa.

Good lines indicate, which are complete, a sign of good character, or normal fate. Their predictions should be precise and easy to do. Again, please understand, these statements are in no way my approval of the tenets of this pseudo-science. I am attempting to pass along the ideas of this system of divination in a fashion that the reader can understand and make a clear judgment of it.

Chapter Thirty-Two:
Runes

Rune (occult) From the German word *naunen*, meaning "secret" or "mystery." It can also mean "whisper." The rune was a MAGIC letter in the early Teutonic alphabet. For WITCHCRAFT a rune is a magical chant. There are various rune alphabets used by OCCULT groups. The runes are ancient Nordic, German or possibly Etruscan alphabets used by some to predict (divination) events in the lives of individuals. It is fortunetelling through casting objects and symbol interpretation. "Each rune not only represents a phonetic sound but also has its own distinct meaning often connected with Norse mythology."37 Runes were the alphabet, but various other meanings were assigned to them for magic or divination. Runic inscriptions can be found everywhere in Scandinavian countries, much like the modern graffiti scattered across the American continent; it is not the alphabet itself that is mystical, although some involved in the occult would argue that point. Whatever its origin, the runes came to be used by some for occult purposes, as a means of fortune-telling, and they are still actively in use today.

Runes also have a very dark period of use during the Second War. Nazi Germany, itself a strongly occultic organism brought runes into everyday daily use in their inordinate desire to reach back into their dark, pagan past to prove that they were "The Master Race." Occult activities were held daily. A rune that all would most likely know by sight, which was the *sig*-rune which was located on the collar of every member of the feared SS. This rune looked like two parallel lightning bolts. It was held to have mystic power and strength to help these savage warriors to carry out their demonic tasks such as administering concentration camps, hunting down "enemies" of the Reich and they were even used as shock-troops in many battles. The SS had a castle where runes were written on the floors, and mystical ceremonies were held in the location. This isn't a commonly known aspect of runes, but they have a dark history indeed.

Chapter Thirty-Three:
Satanism

Of all of the occult practices, although they all to differing degrees worship him, only Satanism directly seeks to have a religious relationship with and worship Satan as a religious entity or idea. Not all Satanists believe that he is an actual individual. Many worship the carnal, masculinity that is part of the physical make-up of the individual. As you might guess, most adherents to this strange religion are young males who claim to be members.

Most Pagans do not address Satan and Wiccans shudder at the idea of doing so. Others strive to be in any sort of relationship that is possible to be in at whatever the cost. Whatever the practice, it is all equally detestable to God. Deuteronomy 18:9-14 tells us,

> *a land wherein thou shalt eat bread without scarceness, thou shalt not lack anything in it; a land whose stones are iron, and out of whose hills thou mayest dig copper. And thou shalt eat and be full, and thou shalt bless Jehovah thy God for the good land which he hath given thee. Beware lest thou forget Jehovah thy God, in not keeping his commandments, and his ordinances, and his statutes, which I command thee this day: lest, when thou halt hast eaten, and art full and hast built goodly houses and dwelt therein; and when thy herds and thy flocks multiply, and thy silver and thy gold is multiplied, and all that thou hast is multiplied; then thy heart be lifted up, and thou forget Jehovah thy God, who brought thee forth out of the land of Egypt, out of the house of bondage.*

It is pretty clear just how much God truly detests these practices and those who practice such things.

"Flavors" of Satanists[23]

Unfortunately, like in worldly Christianity, they are a lot of different types, but we will briefly look at four. **Religious Satanists** (Church of Satan), **Gothic Satanists** (a myth), **Satanic Dabblers**

---

[23] From Wheeler, p. 47.

(experimenting adolescents), and **Quasi-Satanists** (pretenders) will receive a brief examination.

Religious Satanists are from the Church of Satan, the Temple of Set and the Church of the Satanic Liberation. They don't believe in a personal Devil. "Satan" is their term for the force of nature that represents power and sexuality and is derived from the ancient Egyptian deity Set. These names give some the idea that Satanism is an ancient religion, but there are two names (recent, that is) that give it its notoriety. The first was Aleister Crowley and second, was Anton LaVey. These chaps knew how to get noticed and to draw followers.

Crowley (1875-1947) formulated their perversion of the Golden Rule, which was "do what you want to do." He became a famous magician and was ousted from his secret society for homosexuality, drug use, and murder.

LaVey (1930-1997) He was a very accomplished man who was a musician, police photographer, and a circus worker. (See article on "The Satanic Bible" to see him at work in his occupation as a circus worker) He relied on his psychological and magical background to write his "The Satanic Bible." He formed the Church of Satan on April 30, 1966.

There was a division in the Religious Satanic Movement in 1975 when one of the members, Michael Aquino, left the Church of Satan to begin the Temple of Set (ToS). There was no difference in doctrine but disagreement over certain financial agreements. Aquino led defectors, saying that the true ideals of Satanism had been lost. The tradition was correct, just not being followed appropriately. The article mentioned earlier will give a description of the Satanic Bible as well as doctrine as formulated by LaVey. The Church's code of conduct is purely a silly attempt to mock Christianity. There is no depth to the concepts behind the statements. Some ideas attacked are prayer (1 Thessalonians 5:17), turning the other cheek but to retaliate immediately. The "Seven Deadly Sins" (greed, pride, envy, anger, gluttony, lust, and sloth) are encouraged. Sexuality is at the "top of the menu" for Satanist's to partake. Their final rule is that there are no rules. Try to teach that formally!

Satanic Dabblers-young dabblers are extremely self-confident, some say arrogant, and many attribute this to Satan's aggressive personality and correctness as well as his mind-altering abilities. Those personality traits end up being the cause rather than the result of dealing with the evil one. Remember, he hates God and especially his prized creation, humankind. We should expect nothing but his hatred and his willingness to harm us in any possible way that he can. There is no favor from him at all.

Many young Satanic dabblers have emotional problems that lead to their Satanic Involvement. These pre-existing problems will need to be addressed if Satanic involvement is to be resolved. They cannot turn from this mind- controlling doctrine when they find themselves in bondage further to personality disorders or bipolar illnesses.

Quasi-Satanists-They condition is precise as the title indicates. This can be any single or multiple individuals who *think* that they are the good disciples of the Evil one. Any behavior that is in denial to Christianity is seen as right and proper according to their lack-of-values system. A good example of Quasi-Satanists are groups like **Black Sabbath** of the 1970 s, **Alice Cooper**, **Ozzy Osbourne** and so on. A more modern example would be **Marilyn Manson**. These, in other journals, received description as more hard-core Satanists but if you happen to see biographical programs such as on Gene Simmons-the alleged vampire-like leader of the heavy-metal band **KISS**, you see a perfectly normal husband sitting at the morning breakfast table partaking of tea and biscuits. Perfectly normal lives prove that these groups are merely playing a part to sell more albums or perhaps to fill coliseums with fans the next time they pass through town. They are not real-and neither are the fans, who will walk around with face painted white and wearing their favorite artists who sold concert shirts on their last trip through the city. It is all made up like much of Satanism is.

While much of Satanism is made up, there certainly are dangers involved with it. Spiritually, it is absolutely 100% fatal to those involved in it. God sees no "fun" in the running around at nighttime acting as a pagan fool bent upon self-destruction. The emblems of Satanism such as the pentagram are a rejection of God. It scorns Christianity, which is the only way to God. Jesus Christ, The Way, is mocked and scorned. God condemns rebellion as well as involvement with the occult. Remember Samuel's condemnation of both Saul and the Witch of Endor who was both rights amid an occultic ceremony when God brought up Samuel (not the Witch who was more shocked than was Saul who did not know that this was unusual). As he said, Saul was with him in Hades by the next day.

Those who do not believe are lost (Mark 16:15-16). Those who don't obey God will be lost (Ephesians 2:12) One day, every single proponent of Satan will be trembling with fear like the demons did that remembered what was coming their way.

James 2:19 Thou believest that God is one; thou doest well: the demons also believe, and shudder.

We must remember the scripture that says: **Romans 14:10-12** But thou, why dost thou judge thy brother? or thou again, why dost thou set at nought thy brother? for we shall all stand before the judgment-seat of God. For it is written, As I live, saith the Lord, to me every knee shall bow, And every tongue shall confess to God. So then each one of us shall give an account of himself to God. Each of us has some talking to do and we had better get our ducks in order before that day comes!!

When we get that opportunity to worship God, it will be too late to make any fixes!

*2 Corinthians 6:2b behold, now is the acceptable time; behold, **now** is the day of salvation.*

Satanists-what do you want from hell? Admittedly, it can't be much!!

Chapter Thirty-Four:
Spirit Guides

They are also known as spirit-helpers. This is claimed as a spirit/ghost/angel that a spirit medium says is a go-between with the spiritual realm. During what was known as the prime-time of the Spiritualism Church and its subsidiaries, they were well and widely known as a necessary part of the process of communicating with the dearly departed. Some mediums claimed that they needed the intermediates to maintain smooth contact.

Before going further, I would highly suggest reading "**Communicating with the Dead**" to understand where this writer is coming from.

Early Spirit Guides were thought to be Native Americans who had been slaughtered in such large numbers in the recent take-over of the continent. Characters played the part, and it was fashionable to have "an Indian" looking over your shoulder to advise you in your daily dealings. Why he would want to, considering that you- or rather, your people were responsible for the extinction of his people and culture. But, I guess, let bygones be bygones in the afterlife. Also, another little known fact was that no sitter (Medium) was able to utter a single word of Indian language also played into the hands of the mediums tremendously. Books have been written on the tricks and tactics of mediums to carry out their program of deceit and con-jobs. James Randi wrote one that I am presently enjoying. I would consider him as second only to the great Harry Houdini in debunking mediums/spirit-guides etc.

The reason I am so sure as to the fallacy of these "noble creatures" is that according to Jesus Christ himself in Luke 16:19-31, the dead do not roam the spirit world leaving only the demon/evil spirit with the ability to communicate in whatever fashion that they do. Scripture says that some of them are bound in chains of darkness while others, including the god of this world (Satan), wander around from place to place. Look at **Job 1:7**

And Jehovah said unto Satan, Whence comest thou? Then Satan answered Jehovah, and said, From going to and fro in the

earth, and from walking up and down in it. Then afterward:
***Job 2:2** And Jehovah said unto Satan, From whence comest thou? And Satan answered Jehovah, and said, From going to and fro in the earth, and from walking up and down in it.*

Satan says in 2 different places to God that he had been wandering all over the planet so who do you think is doing the communication with these poor duped souls. You see, WE often start our occult career playing with things like Tarot cards, Ouija boards and such like and we END UP being played with by an intelligence far higher than our supposed knowledge. Just because we have the biggest brain on the planet does not assure us of that in the spirit world!

Chapter Thirty-Five:
Tarot Cards

Tarot Cards are a pervasive part of occult theory and practice. They are used by mediums and laypeople equally. Their purpose is divination, or, the foretelling of future events and people.

This is a deck of seventy-eight cards which has various designs on it. It is shuffled, and the cards are laid out and "read' in an attempt to for-tell future events. This is a popular tool that has been used since the 1550 s. There are two different sections, called the *Minor Arcana* and the *Major Arcana*. The *Minor Arcana* consists of 56 cards divided into four suits of fourteen cards: wands, cups, swords, and pentacles. *Major Arcana* consists of 22 cards with individual names and numbers. These are considered the heart of the deck and carry more weight in tarot reading. The *Minor Arcana* deals with the situations of everyday life.

> Divination by some cards is most likely ancient, and scholars claim it was probably practiced in virtually every culture, although there is little proof of this other than the nature of man and his propensity for gaming.

> The modern tarot deck is thought to have descended from an original deck developed as playing cards, with personal and political meanings, for the Italian nobility.42 It came to be known as the Visconti Sforza deck after its creator, Filippo Maria Visconti, who ruled Milan, Italy, from 1412 to 1447. This deck is thought to have developed around 1550 into another popular Italian game called *Tarocchi*. Through the centuries, the card faces were changed more than seven hundred times until they no longer resembled their originals in either meaning or purpose. In the late 1800 s, a resurgence of occult practices focused attention once again on tarot cards, and new, charismatic occult personalities reassigned designs and meanings.

> Tarot has also been associated by some with the Kabbalah Tree of Life, the twenty-two cards somehow corresponding

to "the twenty-two paths on the Tree of Life and, by extension, to the twenty-two letters of the Hebrew alphabet.

The person who becomes involved with tarot readings on any level is looking for a picture of the future. Whoever claims to be able to interpret the cards (very innocent looking on the surface) is saying in reality, "I can tell you something about your future that you do not know." They will point the unsuspecting toward their inner guide" and suggest that mind, soul, and spirit be opened to its direction.

The tarot is an attempt to penetrate beyond this dimension. When people talk about tarot cards, they are discussing a specially designed card believed to hold the key to the future, and to events that influence individual lives.[24]

---

[24] Martin, p. 335.

Chapter Thirty-Six:
The Black Mass

Having written on Satanism and the Satanic Bible previously, I feel somewhat obligated to cover this topic, although it is repulsive to its core. I will try to "dumb it down" and soften the hardness of this repugnant right.

It is said in honor of the Devil at the witch's sabbath. Many Satanic groups practice it. The primary purpose is to mock the Roman Catholic mass in every way possible, desecrating the objects they use in ritual. Often, a nude woman is used as the altar with the priest having sexual relations with her and the end of the ceremony.

Sometimes the blood of an animal is drunk, and human flesh is eaten during this mockery of all that is holy. Human sacrifices are not unknown during these times.

The black mass contains many other repulsive practices that are unmentionable. It perverts and desecrates the true worship of God and is a blasphemous insult to all believers in Christ.

Clifford Wilson and John Weldon described a black mass as follows:

Normally, a small group of people sit in front of a table covered with a purple velvet altar cloth, lit with candles. Over the "altar" hangs a cross upside down and a picture of the devil, half-human, half-beast. A high priest stands by the table dressed in bishop's robes. On his person, he wears an inverted cross. He throws a larger cross to the floor. "Shemhaforash," he shouts. This is probably the most powerful word uttered in satanic worship. According to the Talmud (a book of Jewish civil and religious laws and ethical lore), it was the secret mystic word spoken by God when He created the world. He then spits upon the cross, with an obscene gesture, and cries, "Hail Satan!" Thus begins the sickening and blasphemous ritual, as the devil worshippers repeat the Lord's prayer backwards and make a mockery of the ordinances of the church. One quotation from LaVey's "The Satanic Bible" says, "Blessed are the strong, for they shall possess the earth." "If a man smites you on one cheek, smash him on the other!"

Nudity is commonly found at satanic covens. When a witch is initiated, she is symbolically "sacrificed" to the sun god, and this ceremony takes place while she is lying naked on the altar. The power of the witch is said to be heightened by the mysterious force that is within her own body, and when clothing is worn that power is supposedly obstructed. Their delusion is that they will gain pleasure and enjoyment in this world, especially of a sensual nature and that in a coming age Satan will overcome the Christians' God and return to the heaven from which he was once thrown out. Satan's earthly followers, so the delusion goes, will then share fruits of eternal power with his spirit forces.[25]

Such wickedness is often looked upon as merely "free speech in religion" these days, but we have to see it as it is, an outright attempt to be as blasphemous to our Holy God and all those involved will answer for as well as to pay for this affront at all that is called holy. I am not speaking of the Roman Catholic Ceremonies for they are just that-man-made ceremonies, but the spiritual contempt for God's holy ways will be answered for. A day will come when even Satan, his demons, and those who are bound in the occult will no longer celebrate the black mass but will be forced to bow to the Lord Jesus Christ.

> *Philippians 2:10-11 that in the name of Jesus every knee should bow, of things in heaven and things on earth and things under the earth, and that every tongue should confess that Jesus Christ is Lord, to the glory of God the Father.*

---

[25] Clifford Wilson and John Weldon, *Occult Shock and Psychic Forces,* San Diego: Master Books, 1980, pp. 9, 10

Chapter Thirty-Seven:
The Nature, and Character of Demons

The Origin of Demons

The origin of the word "demon" is somewhat obscure, coming from the Greek word daimonion or "to know." Among pagan Greeks, an inferior deity, whether good or bad. In the New Testament, it denotes "an evil spirit."[26]

There are some who claim that they are the disembodied spirits of a pre-Adamic race of men who lived on the earth in a gap period which supposedly occurred between Genesis 1:1-1:2. There are two problems with that idea. 1) There were no men before Adam, 2) When men die, they go right to paradise/torment before judgment, not galloping around the world doing evil. (See Communicating with the Dead)

Others claim that demons are the result of cohabitation between women and angels in the pre-flood world. (Genesis 6:1-6) This theory is "blown out of the water" by Christ when he stated that angels are sexless beings, incapable of such unions (Matthew 22:30)

Another view was that they were the spirits of the wicked dead men who were allowed by God to leave the Hadean realm to accommodate the plan of salvation. Kind of a "get out of jail" card to help the Lord out, if you can believe that. Josephus claimed that demons were the "spirits of wicked men" that enter into men that were alive and kill them unless they can obtain some help against them.

The last, most likely argument was that the first century demons were to be identified with the fallen angels of 2 Peter 2:4 and Jude verse 6, some of whom were allowed to leave that confinement for inhabiting certain people. Charles Hodge held to this theory, which is probably the most popular of all the theories.

---

[26] Vine, p. 157.

Ultimately, there is no scriptural explanation for the matter, and it falls into the realm of silence. Since there is no explanation, let us "Speak where the Bible speaks and be silent where the Bible is silent."

The Nature and Character of Demons

The New Testament is obvious in the nature of demons. They are reported to be pure spirits. Matthew says in 8:16: And when even was come, they brought unto him many possessed with demons: and he cast out the spirits with a word and healed all that were sick. Here the NT uses the term "demon" and "spirit" interchangeably showing the nature to be the same.

As spirit beings, we could see different aspects of their natures. Matthew 12:44-45 volition ("I will return...".) locomotion ("Then goeth he...") shows these two aspects of their being. They can desire to go and then do it. Another thing is that they can assimilate factual information. At one time, a demon once said to Christ, "I know thee who thou art, the Holy One of God."(Luke4:34, Mark 1:24) They also possessed a religious sensitivity, "Thou believest that God is one; thou doest well, the demons also believe and shudder." "Shudder-*phrisso*-to be rough, to bristle" then to "shiver, shudder, tremble." (Vines 1985, 573) They are very frightened as to their ultimate doom. (and they should be)

Character is a little bit to dig into. They are depicted as "unclean" and "evil." Matthew 12:43-45 tells us that:

> *But the unclean spirit, when he is gone out of the man, passeth through waterless places, seeking rest, and findeth it not. Then he saith, I will return into my house whence I came out; and when he comes, he findeth it empty, swept, and garnished. Then goeth he, and taketh with himself seven other spirits more evil than himself, and they enter in and dwell there: and the last state of that man becometh worse than the first. Even so, shall it be also unto this evil generation?*

The spirit left the man and after some thought decided to return to his former dwelling place taking with him several, "more evil" companions so that the last state of the man was worst off than the first. From this text, we learn that there are various "levels" of vileness.

Demon Possession

Demon possession is such a flaming hot, controversial issue that has been ignited inside as well as outside of the church. Saints AND sinners are well prepared to carry the banner of their particular party when it comes to this issue. There are very few who are not in favor of one way or the other. Why I do not know, but it just is that way.

The differences between possession in the New Testament and in our time are very great indeed, and an argument which I feel is the correct one comes from Zechariah. The New Testament is evident in its teaching that there was going to be a day when the era of the miraculous was going to end. When miracles ended, the case of the causes was going to come to a close as well.

> **Zechariah 13:1-2** *In that day there shall be a fountain opened to the house of David and to the inhabitants of Jerusalem, for sin and for uncleanness. And it shall come to pass in that day, saith Jehovah of hosts, that I will cut off the names of the idols out of the land, and they shall no more be remembered, and also I will cause the prophets and the unclean spirit to pass out of the land.*

In this, "unclean spirit" is pretty clear and specific. There are those who feel that this is THE answer but also those who are firmly against the idea, and those are the folks who tend to say that demons are still amongst the people. It pivots over the point there.

If you are to take the issue of the demonic ejection, you can compare between the two times. How was it accomplished is very different? In N.T. times, it was performed by speaking the word of God like Jesus, Paul, or even, at the far end of the scale, the sons of Sceva, the priest.

> *Acts 19:14-20 And there were seven sons of one Sceva, a Jew, a chief priest, who did this. And the evil spirit answered and said unto them, Jesus I know, and Paul I know; but who are ye? And the man in whom the evil spirit was leaped on them, and mastered both of them, and prevailed against them so that they fled out of that house naked and wounded. And this became known to all, both Jews and Greeks, that dwelt at Ephesus; and fear fell upon them all, and the name of the Lord Je-*

177

sus was magnified. Many also of them that had believed came, confessing, and declaring their deeds. And not a few of them that practised magical arts brought their books together and burned them in the sight of all, and they counted the price of them and found it fifty thousand pieces of silver. So mightily grew the word of the Lord and prevailed.

I realize that I went a little far in dealing with those who cast out demons by speech, but you can see where they (the sons of Sceva) were attempting to carry this out in their everyday occupation; in verse thirteen they were referred to as "strolling Jews" and cast demons forth by their manner of speech which was "piggy-backing" off of the faith of the real exorcists-the apostles of Christ.

Homer Hailey, in his excellent commentary, has to say

> "An apostate church could yield to forms of idolatry, but the true church would not. True prophets would pass out of the land, but false prophets would not, for these may ever plague the church. True prophets would cease, for there would no longer be a need for them. Prophets were inspired teachers, often identified in the New Testament with the apostles, assisting in the laying of the foundation of the church and the completing of revelation (Eph. 2:20; 3:5; 4:11). Once the foundation was laid and the new revelation was complete, the need for prophets would cease. Daniel indicates the same in a strong Messianic prophecy, when he said of the anointed one, the prince, that He would "bring in everlasting righteousness," and "seal up vision and prophecy [prophet, margin, ASV]." Likewise, unclean spirits, the antithesis of the prophets, would cease. In the conquest of Christ over Satan and his forces, unclean spirits have ceased to control men as they did in the time of the ministry of Christ and the apostles (cf. also Mic. 5:12-13).[27]

This isn't a standard view of Zechariah but is still a usable piece of Scripture.

The Lord and His disciples could eject an evil spirit with a simple word, but can a disciple do so today? Also, exorcisms were

---

[27] Homer Hailey, *The Minor Prophets*, p. 392.

done in wide-open, public areas back in those times. Are these done in the same methods as were practiced back in those days? What about the technique used? The same or different?

Today, they appear in dark out-of-the-way places that are hidden from all, but the most ardent followers as the song say, back alley, trusty woods. There you will find them. In New Testament times, it was not hidden. It was dealt with when and where it occurred. As an example, look at Paul's dealings with the slave girl that followed them for days telling everyone around them that they were servants of the most-high God. Paul did not want to advertise from a demonically possessed girl and brought the advertising to an end. Acts 16:17. Everyone knew about the Gadarene demoniac that Jesus healed. It was no big secret but something that society dealt with because it had to. Today, you might hear of a rumor of an exorcism, but that is about all. Faith healers often use supposed "demoniacs" in their healing shows, but these individuals are not what a demon possessed person is. Those "healing shows" end up being a complete and total sham in all of their ways. They honor and glorify a man-the supposed "healer" and not God; the one who deserves to be honored in every way possible.

Finally, there are no modern-day possessions because the reason that possessions were allowed in New Testament times was to show the power of Christ and his apostles. They are no longer with us, and the reason for possession no longer exists.

What we see today as demon possession is demon subjection. Demons are not in the person possessing them but are controlling them by subjection to the demonic will. Christ is not going to allow Satan to gain power over mankind when there is no way of protecting his servants from him. The apostles with their apostolic power are gone, so is the evil spirit (returning to Zechariah 13:1-2).

Chapter Thirty-Eight:
The Ouija Board Examined

The Ouija board also is called a "spirit" or "talking" board. In its commercial release, consisting of a wooden board marked with the alphabet, numbers from 0-9, the words "yes" or "no," "hello" and "goodbye," and has various symbols and graphics on the board. Along with it is a small piece of wood or plastic, called a "planchette." that the participants place their fingers on it and ask a question. The planchette will begin slowly to move but will, with practice speed up until it answers questions with speed. A conversation, asking questions, will then be carried on with great "normality" causing most participants to be at ease and will allow the board to answer very personal matters of all types.

The Ouija board is an old "toy" gameboard that was introduced commercially by a businessman named Elijah Bond back on July 1, 1890. At first, it was seen as a parlor game unrelated to any occult activity. During the First World War, an American spiritualist by the name of Pearl Curran popularized Ouija as a divining tool. Before that, spiritualists claimed that they were able to use the board to contact the dead while they were in their spiritualist camps in Ohio in 1886. (This one fact shows that homemade boards were being made and used at a much earlier date than the commercially made boards.)

Ouija boards have a long history starting back during the Song Dynasty in China around 1100 AD. It is found in historical documents and was called "Fuji" or "planchette writing." The use of planchette writing as an ostensible means of necromancy and communion with the spirit-world was continued, and, under special rituals and supervisions, was a central practice of the Quanzhen School, until it was forbidden by the Qing Dynasty. Several entire scriptures of the Daozang are supposedly works of automatic planchette writing.

Although Ouija boards are very popular in today's society, warnings can be heard by those in psychological as well as religious fields. The psychological is concerned about personality issues while the religious leaders are concerned about demon-impression leading to attacks upon persons and players of this "wonderful board game."

Ouija boards were already criticized by scholars early on, is described in a 1927 journal as "'vestigial remains' of primitive belief-systems" and a con to part fools from their money. Another 1921 journal described reports of Ouija board findings as half-truths' and suggested that their inclusion in national newspapers at the time lowered the national discourse overall

In the 1970 s Ouija board users were also described as "cult members" by sociologists, though those in the field severely condemned this

Since early in the Ouija board's history, it has been criticized by several Christian denominations. For example, *Catholic Answers*, a Roman Catholic Christian apologetics organization, states that "The Ouija board is far from harmless, as it is a form of divination (seeking information from supernatural sources)." Moreover, Catholic Christian bishops in Micronesia called for the boards to be banned and warned congregations that they were talking to demons when using Ouija boards. In a pastoral letter, The Dutch Reformed Churches encouraged its communicants to avoid Ouija boards, as it is a practice "related to the occult." The Wisconsin Evangelical Lutheran Synod also forbids its faithful from using Ouija boards as it teaches that such would be a violation of the Ten Commandments.

In 2001, Ouija boards were burned in Alamogordo, New Mexico, by fundamentalist groups alongside *Harry Potter* books as "symbols of witchcraft." Religious criticism has also expressed beliefs that the Ouija board reveals information which should only be in God's hands, and thus, it is a tool of Satan. A spokesperson for Human Life International described the boards as a portal to talk to spirits and called for Hasbro to be prohibited from marketing them

These religious objections to using the Ouija board have in turn given rise to <u>ostension</u> type <u>folklore</u> in the communities where they circulate. <u>Cautionary tales</u> that the board opens the door to evil spirits turn the game into the subject of a supernatural dare, especially for young people.[28]

There are several later users whom it would be interesting to note who they were. The first being none other than Aleister Crowley, (an early Satanist) who was quoted as saying

Your Ouija board experiment is rather fun. You see how very satisfactory it is, but I believe things improve greatly with practice. I think you should keep to one angel and make the magical preparations more elaborate." A few years later: Re: Ouija Board. I offer you the basis of ten percent of my net profit. You are if you accept this, responsible for the legal protection of the ideas, and the marketing of the copyright designs. I trust that this may be satisfactory for you. I hope to let you have the material in the course of a week." Finally: There is, however, a good way of using this instrument to get what you want, and that is to perform the whole operation in a consecrated circle so that undesirable aliens cannot interfere with it. You should then employ the proper magical invocation to get into your circle just the one spirit you want. It is comparatively easy to do this. A few simple instructions are all that is necessary, and I shall be pleased to give these, free of charge, to anyone who cares to apply.

What a guy, huh?

In popular culture: Ouija boards have figured prominently in horror tales in various media as devices enabling malevolent spirits to spook their users. Most often, they make brief appearances, relying heavily on the atmosphere of mystery the board already holds in the mind of the viewer, to add credence to the paranormal presence in the story being told.

In the movie ***Paranormal Activity*** (2007) involves a violent entity haunting a couple that becomes more powerful when the Ouija

---

[28] https://en.wikipedia.org/wiki/Ouija

board is used. Another 2007 film, **_Ouija_**, depicted a group of adolescents whose use of the board causes a murderous spirit to follow them, while four years later, **_The Ouija Experiment_** portrayed a group of friends whose use of the board opens, and fails to close, a portal between the worlds of the living and the dead. Now, exactly what these child's toys open or close doors is uncertain, but those who have used them-this writer included-do know that something happens which we cannot undo. Be it a door, window, or merry-go-round; something does happen that we cannot control. It is best to stay away from it and stay close to God. The Ouija does something that we can't undo. Be ye warned!!!

Chapter Thirty-Nine:
The Satanic Bible

One day, it occurred to me that I had an unusual opportunity that not many Christians have. I was not overly excited by the prospect but decided that I needed to do my very best with the opportunity I had. What I am referring to is to write a description for my brethren about what is in the so-called "Satanic Bible." I was attempting to gain an understanding of what is involved in the Occult movement. This, unfortunately, is growing in strength and popularity in our ever-more sickening culture. Before I begin, I do want to explain that I have mixed emotions when looking at this "work." It is a mixture of nausea and disgust. You will understand after the series is complete.

I will make all statements and quotes from the book in italics (similar to how I quote scripture in other articles) or parenthesis marks to set it apart from my comments. I will let the book speak for itself and attempt not to let my personal revulsion in any way color my reporting to you.

This particular copy is a paperback published by Avon Books. It is obviously a paperback knock-off rather than what one would imagine; like perhaps, an old, leather-bound hardback book with parchment pages, marked by candle-wax drippings from some dark secret midnight ceremony. Uh-uh. This is trade paperback book, packaged to meet the masses. That is the problem-*for the masses*. Part of the introduction: Called "The Black Pope" by many of his followers, Anton LaVey began the road to High Priesthood of the Church of Satan when he was only 16 years old and an organ player in a carnival.

> On Saturday night I would see men lusting after half-naked girls dancing at the carnival, and on Sunday morning when I was playing the organ for tent-show evangelists at the other end of the carnival lot, I would see these same men sitting in the pews with their wives and children, asking God to forgive them and purge them of carnal desires. And the next Saturday night they'd be back at the carnival or

some other place of indulgence." "I knew then that the Christian Church thrives on hypocrisy, and that man's carnal nature will win out!" and "Since worship of fleshly things produces pleasure, there would then be a temple of glorious indulgence..."

The book begins with "The Nine Satanic Statements

1) Satan represents indulgence instead of abstinence!
2) Satan represents vital existence instead of spiritual pipe dreams!
3) Satan represents undefiled wisdom instead of hypocritical *self-deceit*!
4) Satan represents kindness to those who deserve it, instead of love wasted on ingrates!
5) Satan represents vengeance, instead of turning the other cheek!
6) Satan represents responsibility to the responsible, instead of concern for psychic vampires!
7) Satan represents man as just another animal, sometimes better, more often worse than those that walk on all-fours, who, because of his "divine spiritual and intellectual development," has become the most vicious animal of all!
8) Satan represents all of the so-called sins, as they all lead to physical, mental, or emotional gratification!
9) Satan has been the best friend the church has ever had, as he has kept it in business all these years!"

I will give the table of contents which will give the reader an idea of what is in this book. As often stated in witchcraft, it follows closely the ideas of Earth, Air, Fire, and Water. Book One is: **(Fire)—The Book of Satan—The Infernal Diatribe**. This part begins with:

> "The first book of the Satanic Bible is not an attempt to blaspheme as much as it is a statement of what might be termed "diabolical indignation." The Devil has been attacked by the men of God relentlessly and without reservation. Never has there been an opportunity, short of fiction, for the Dark Prince to speak out in the same manner as the spokesmen of the Lord of the Righteous..."

(Air)—Book of Lucifer—The Enlightenment. This book begins with:

> "The Roman god, Lucifer, the bearer of light, the spirit of the air, the personification of enlightenment. In Christian mythology, he became synonymous with evil, which was only to have been expected from a religion whose very existence is perpetuated by clouded definitions and bogus values! It is time to set the record straight. False moralisms and inaccuracies must be corrected...."

(Earth)—Book of Belial—The Mastery of the Earth.

> "The greatest appeal of magic is not in its application but its esoteric meanderings. The element of mystery which so enshrouds the practice of the black arts has been fostered, deliberately or out of ignorance, by those who often claim the highest expertise in such matters...."

(Water)—Book of Leviathan—The Raging Sea.

> "Despite all non-verbalists protests to the contrary, soaring heights of emotional ecstasy or raging pangs of anguish can be attained through verbal communication. If the magical ceremony is to employ all sensory awarenesses, then the proper sounds must be invoked. It is certainly true that "actions speak louder than words," but words became as monuments to thoughts...."

It has an "Invocation to Satan" which is full of bluff and blunder and of lies, which according to our Lord-THE TRUE LORD-is his native language. Jesus said:

> *You are of your father the devil, and your will is to do your father's desires. He was a murderer from the beginning and had nothing to do with the truth because there is no truth in him. When he lies, he speaks out of his own character, for he is a liar and the father of lies.*

The book is full of all sorts of lies and deception as one would expect from a document of this type. The saddest thing about this is that the folks who embrace this "theology" do not realize that they are being lied to the most and that the "Lord and Master" that they believe will lead them to victory is a defeated criminal on the way to the gallows. They have nothing to look forward to besides eternity in the Lake of Fire. How truly sad it is. Jesus died for them as well and God loves them and has made the utmost effort to save them from their sins. I suspect that the "weeping and gnashing of teeth" will be from these folks who will deeply, <u>deeply</u> regret the decision they made and that they believed a lie and have all eternity to regret it!! We need to pray for these people day and night because they need it-probably more than most!![29]

In a further article, I will give a short history of Satanism and its adherents. It is important that we know some of what the enemy is doing so that we may be better servants, more prepared to do the will of our Father.

Soli Deo Gloria!--To God alone is the glory!!!

---

[29] Anton Szandor LaVey.

Chapter Forty:
Warfare in the Spiritual
and Physical Realms

It is essential for us to know that warfare did not start in this earthly realm but began in Heaven when approximately one-third (see Rev. 12:4) of the angels rose in the rebellion of their leader, the one who came to be known as Satan and the Devil.

> *Revelation 12:7-9 And there was war in heaven: Michael and his angels going forth to war with the dragon; and the dragon warred and his angels; and they prevailed not, neither was their place found any more in heaven. And the great dragon was cast down, the old serpent, he that is called the Devil and Satan, the deceiver of the whole world; he was cast down to the earth, and his angels were cast down with him.*

We learn in **2 Peter 2:4** that:

> *For if God spared not angels when they sinned, but cast them down to hell, and committed them to pits of darkness, to be reserved unto judgment.*

There was no redemption provided for them. Why we were not told.

We learn from two verses that Jesus dealt with Satan before he came to earth:

> *Luke 10:18: And he said unto them, I beheld Satan fallen as lightning from heaven.*

The other verse is **Revelation 12:7-9** (quoted above). These tell us that Jesus was there, as they have said, "taking care of business."

The warfare of the spiritual variety was introduced to our physical world early in its existence. This began when Satan, using the form of a serpent, tempted our first parents and caused them to sin and fall under his sway. God, in Genesis 3:15, made a prophecy of the world's redemption and Satan to be destroyed here as well. Sin was introduced into the world, and warfare continued on in that

188

manner. It was not long until the first murder, and all sorts of other foul behaviors such as polygamy and every possible wrong flooded the globe, causing God to destroy it with a flood to start over. In the time continuum, characters like Enoch, Seth, and Abraham come along, showing that righteousness was possible and that one was not bound to follow the path of sin. God showed hope and promise with these.

Now that we come to the nation of Israel, we come to both spiritual and physical war. Physical war is a result of sin, and sin is the result of our sinful hearts being "aided" by those in the realm of darkness. All in all, God has made the way of salvation available through the sacrifice of His Son, so we need not serve sin in the form of the world, the flesh, and the Devil. They can and will be defeated in the lives of those of us who seek to obey Him and walk in fellowship with Him. That is the spiritual war that we each face. Hopefully, our mature relationship with God is going to preclude any carnal, or physical battles in the lives of us all. Our kingdom is not of this world, and hence we should put that first above carnal warfare as it is waged in this world.

> *Matt. 6:33 But seek ye first his kingdom, and his righteousness, and all these things shall be added unto you.*

Spiritual warfare is to carry on in the lives of His children. We are here living in enemy territory, and conflict will certainly arise. In 2 Corinthians 10:3-5 we read:

> *For though we walk in the flesh, we do not war according to the flesh (for the weapons of <u>our warfare</u> are not of the flesh, but mighty before God to the casting down of strongholds), casting down imaginations, and every high thing that is exalted against the knowledge of God, and bringing every thought into captivity to the obedience of Christ.*

There is going to be war, and the next verses tell us how this spiritual war is to be conducted:

> **Eph. 6:10-16** *Finally, be strong in the Lord, and in the strength of his might. Put on the whole armor of God, that ye may be able to stand against the wiles of the devil. For our wrestling is not against flesh and blood, but against the prin-*

cipalities, against the powers, against the world-rulers of this darkness, against the spiritual hosts of wickedness in the heavenly places. Wherefore take up the whole armor of God, that ye may be able to withstand in the evil day, and, having done all, to stand. Stand therefore, having girded your loins with truth, and having put on the breastplate of righteousness, and having shod your feet with the preparation of the gospel of peace; withal taking up the shield of faith, wherewith ye shall be able to quench all the fiery darts of the evil one. And take the helmet of salvation, and the sword of the Spirit, which is the word of God: with all prayer and supplication praying at all seasons in the Spirit, and watching thereunto in all perseverance and supplication for all the saints.

So, after we read these two sections of scriptures, we learn a great number of things. It is *our battle,* and we must participate. It is here in this world, where we are. It is mighty power that we are given for casting down strongholds of the enemy. (that is why I named this book **Casting Down of Strongholds**—it is to guide the reader out from under the thralldom of the occult and to lift you to the point to where you can blast the enemy using God's authoritative word.) Having access to God's weaponry is to have access to Ephesians 6:10-18 and to use it rightly.

We are to put on and use the whole armor of God in **verse eleven** so that we can stand against the Devil's wiles.

In **verse twelve**, we learn of who is our actual opponent. The Devil is over an army, and we are facing that army.

Verse thirteen again a reminder to stand. It only takes God saying something once. What could it mean if he says it twice in three verses? **Verse fourteen** tells us that it is the truth—John 8:32: *and ye shall know the truth, and the truth shall make you free.* That makes us free. Lies enslave us and lies are the language of the enemy:

John 8:44 Ye are of your father, the devil, and the lusts of your father it is your will to do. He was a murderer from the beginning, and standeth not in the truth, because there is no truth in him. When he speaketh a lie, he speaketh of his own: for he is a liar, and the father thereof.

Stay away from lies; they are an attack of the devil. **Verse sixteen** tells us about the shield of faith, that protect us from flaming darts. Our hope is the victory that overcomes the world! It is a powerful shield to protect us. We must use it if we are to survive in this war. **Verse seventeen,** tells us about the helmet of salvation (assurance of salvation) and then the MIGHTY Sword-the Word of God. With that, you can strike down all liars and evildoers. God's word is our only offensive weapon, but it is far more than we could hope to need. Learn it, live it.

Verse eighteen speaks of prayer and supplication as last but not least. We are to 1 Thessalonians 5:17 *pray without ceasing;* talk to God about it and what can be done with it, saved or not. That is the key-the word of God and prayer. That will rescue any hostage, drive away bandits and ne'er-do-wells. Learn to live this lifestyle, and God will help and strengthen any weak soldier and prepare him for honor and glory in his service. Finally, returning to verse eleven: *be strong in the Lord, and in the strength of his might.* If this is the first time that you have read this book: consider yourself on the road to education and in the Lord's Army!!

Bibliography

Christian Counseling—Koch
Spiritual Warfare—Ray C. Sted
Teach Them About Satan—Lovett
In the Name of Satan—Larson
Praying the Psalms for Spiritual Warfare—Dr. A.O. Itola
Demonic Possession in the New Testament—W.M. Alexander
The Gospel Versus Occultism—Conley
The Pagan Book of Days—Pennick
Deliverance from Evil Spirits—Macnutt
Kingdom of the Occult—Walter Martin
Dictionary of Cults, Sects, Religions and the Occult—Nichols and
    Mather
The Encyclopedia of Occult Sciences—Tudor
Biblical Demonology—Unger
Principalities and Powers—Bethany
Resist Satan—Rob Harbison
Devils, Demons and Deliverance— Hickey
What Demons Can Do to Saints—Unger
Mind Games—Andre Kole
The Occults—V.E. Howard
An Encyclopedia of Claims, Frauds, and Hoaxes of the Occult and
    Supernatural—James Randi
Dispelling the Darkness—Greg Harmon
Encyclopedia of the Bible—Zondervan
Int'l Standard Bible Encyclopedia
Encyclopedia of the Stone Campbell Mvmnt.
Beyond Death's Door—Owen Olbricht
The Satanic Bible—LaVey

.

Made in the USA
Lexington, KY
06 November 2019